BUILD BLOCKS

PIECES OF ENCOURAGEMENT
FOR THE JOURNEY OF FAITH

Peace be with you
Christy

CHRISTY YOUNGBLOOD DESISTO

23 Penguins Publications
Westford, MA

First printing, November, 2009

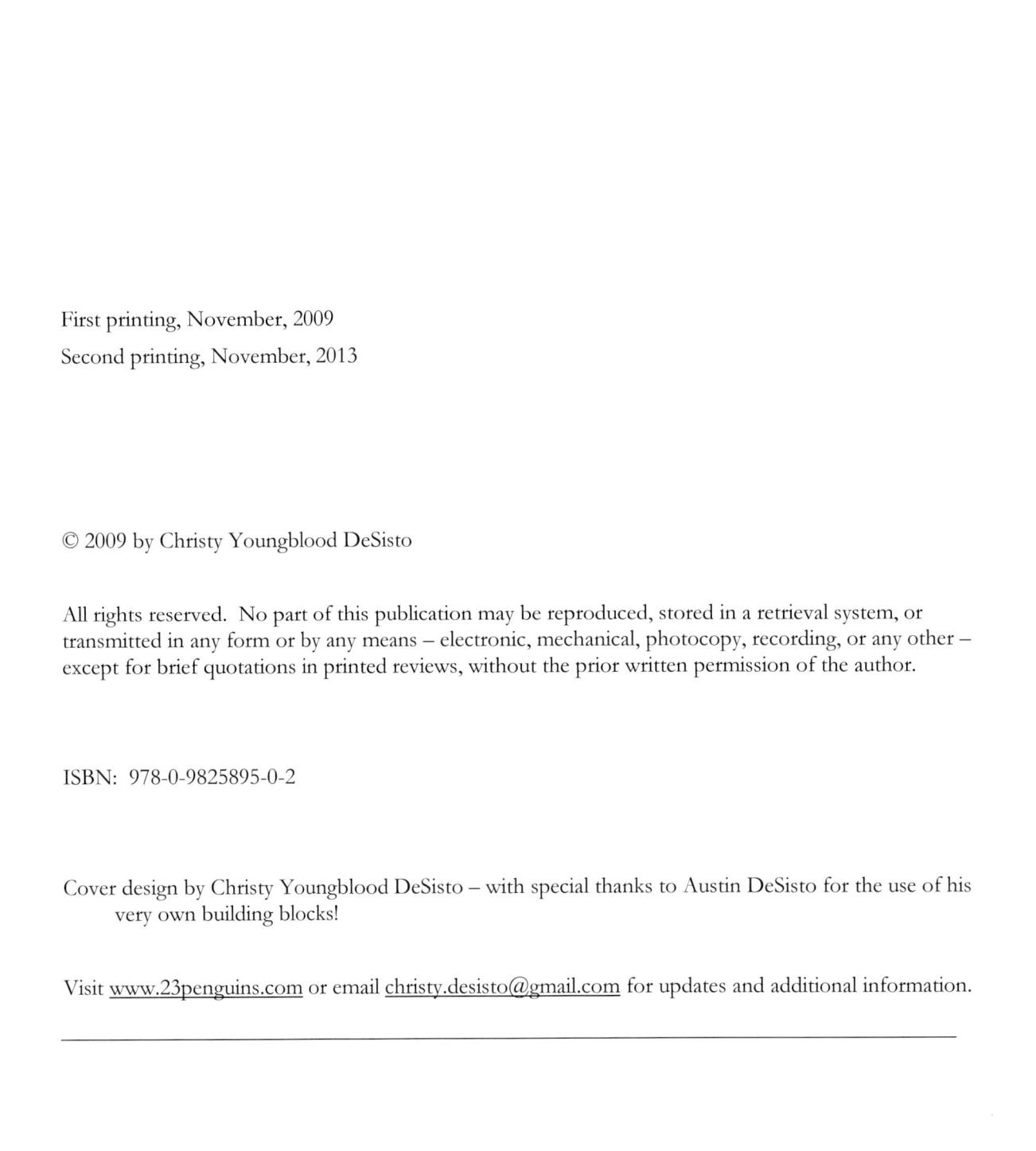

Second printing, November, 2013

© 2009 by Christy Youngblood DeSisto

All rights reserved. No part of this publication may be reproduced, stored in a retrieval system, or transmitted in any form or by any means – electronic, mechanical, photocopy, recording, or any other – except for brief quotations in printed reviews, without the prior written permission of the author.

ISBN: 978-0-9825895-0-2

Cover design by Christy Youngblood DeSisto – with special thanks to Austin DeSisto for the use of his very own building blocks!

Visit www.23penguins.com or email christy.desisto@gmail.com for updates and additional information.

This book is dedicated to:

Building Blocks Subscribers and Readers
*Who through the years have provided constant
feedback and encouragement*

Rob, Robbo, and Austin
*Three incredible blessings from God!
Words are not adequate to express how much I love you…*

Table of Contents

Preface		Time to Surrender	29
The Pilot's Voice	1	In Unexpected Ways	31
Peppering the Cake	3	Admission to Worship	33
Getting Noticed	6	Yesterday and Today	35
The "Things We're Good At"	8	The Stretching Question	37
Learn to Be Still	10	Reliving Mistakes	39
A Prayer of Thanksgiving	13	Even If	41
Snuggle Time	15	For All People	43
The Roller Coaster Life	17	Push and Pull	45
Light and Dark	19	These Days	47
Day-to-Day	21	An Evening Prayer for Those We Love	50
No Longer Condemned	23	Treasures Among the Trash	51
The Oasis	25	Trusting the Process	53
"God" Friends	27	Leaves	55

Stripes	57	Blankie	97
Stripes, Part 2	59	Snow Farms	99
Imitators All	61	Circle Up	101
Receiving Love	63	Jump Practice	103
Who's Cool	66	Wide Awake	105
Breathe	68	Keep Shooting the Ball	107
Credit Who?	71	Getting Back on the Plane	110
Pleasure and Pain	73	Chosen	113
When the Lights Go Down	75	Deeper Still	115
Words	77	Elbow Room	117
Everything We Need	79	A Goofy Investment	119
The Basics	81	Forcing the Issue	121
Passion, Anyone?	83	Outside the Comfort Zone	123
Once Upon a Time	85	Letter to Santa	125
Second-Guessing	87	Bird by Bird	127
Struggling to Learn	90	The Presence of God	129
Been There, Done That	92	The Script	132
The Only Day	94	Never Too Late	135

This Too Shall Pass	137	The Wax Team	163
Getting In First	139	The Signature of God	165
The First Move	141	Grace and Love	167
The "Bug in the Basement"	143	Smile for the Camera!	169
What You Got	145	Prayer for Stillness	171
Looking and Moving	147	Remember	173
A Coach's Words	149	A Balloon Called Anger	175
Drawing Straws	151	Nothing Wasted	177
"Paw-Prints" of God	153	Coming Home	179
The Real Deal	155	The Question of Pain	181
Enough	157	The Receiving End of Injustice	183
Compassion in the "Swarm"	159	Standards of Measurement	186
Over-the-Hill	161	Topical Index	189

Preface

The book you hold in your hands is a selected group of daily devotionals that I have written and distributed to subscribers via email over the past few years.

Believe it or not, my decision to begin writing daily devotionals was born out of a painful experience. I was a minister at Riverbend Church in Austin, Texas, at the time, and the email media was still relatively young for the population at-large. But I started writing, and as Riverbend tended to always be on the cutting-edge, we offered the daily devotionals via an email distribution format. Surprisingly, within only a few weeks, we had substantial subscriber list!

In the spring of 2001, I began contemplating making a move to Boston. In the summer, it became a reality. I sold my house and car, left a well-paid position at Riverbend for a $9/hour job at a residential treatment center for adolescent girls, drove 2000 miles in a Ryder truck with a drugged-up cat, and moved into a 400-square-foot brownstone apartment in the Fenway neighborhood of Boston. The only way to explain such craziness? God.

Riverbend was gracious (and perhaps needed a daily writer enough!) to provide me with a monthly stipend to continue writing the devotionals long-distance. But at the beginning of the new budget year, the funds became no longer available. So "One Step Closer" – as the devotionals were then known – came to an end.

I enjoyed writing too much, however. I was challenged – not only by the process and the daily deadlines, but by the continual quest to look for and find God in the everyday situations of life. And I wasn't sure that I was ready to stop just yet.

So with Riverbend's permission, I polled their subscribers and began a new list for those who wanted to receive future devotionals that I would continue to author and distribute independently. Thus, began Building Blocks.

I set up my own website, distribution list, and went to work. Many readers were quick to respond not only with verbal encouragement, but also with financial support in the early Building Blocks days. I continually felt affirmed both in my writing itself and in the decision that I had made to continue.

Building Blocks has been a wonderful journey, albeit not the most consistent one. About a year after I landed in Boston, I met a wonderful man and his 6-year-old son, who had lost their wife & mom a year earlier to breast cancer. The last thing I was looking for was a relationship, but as they say… "the rest is history." What an amazing blessing they are to me!

One of the things I discovered, is that if I thought finding time to write as a single person was difficult, it couldn't compare to finding time to write while taking care of a family – especially when Austin came along! While I tried to continue writing daily, eventually I had to admit that recycling previously written devotionals wasn't fair to anyone, and my frustration over not being able to create new material was over-the-top. So I finally took a sabbatical that continues to this day.

I can't say if and when I will pick up the daily devotional-writing routine or not. For now, it is my hope that the collection here will encourage and give you hope along your journey. They are simple offerings born out of everyday life and experiences. May you hear God whisper his words of love to you among its pages.

Christy

The Pilot's Voice

"For he is our God. We are the people he watches over, the sheep under his care.

Oh, that you would listen to his voice today!"

Psalm 95:7

The seven-year-old was just beginning to process bits and pieces of 9/11, which he had been sheltered from, as he was only five when it happened. It brought up all kinds of questions and concerns for the young boy and his upcoming plane trip, not the least of which was, "Can that happen on our flight?"

After talking about things a bit with his parents, his fears seemed to subside for the most part. When they began their trip a couple of days later, the excitement of the journey overshadowed any anxiety he had experienced. After making a connection in Atlanta, their plane taxied to the runway, but as always the case in Atlanta, there was a long line for takeoff.

The boy's anxiety began to grow and he popped off rapid-fire questions: "Why isn't the pilot talking to us? He usually tells us what number we are for take-off. How come he hasn't said anything yet?" A few minutes later, the voice from the cockpit did welcome everyone aboard and revealed the pecking order.

The boy turned and grinned and said to his mom, "Now that I've heard his voice, I'm not worried anymore. I just needed to hear the pilot's voice."

The seven-year-old may well speak for all of us. How often do we just need to hear the Pilot's voice to calm our fears?

In this journey we call life, there are many things that happen along the way that cause us to fear. Things that make us worry. Things that are beyond our control. Things that leave us paralyzed with our hearts in our throats.

At these times, may we remember to listen for the calming, reassuring voice of God.

Peppering the Cake

"But remember that the temptations that come into your life are no different from what others experience. And God is faithful. He will keep the temptation from becoming so strong that you can't stand up against it. When you are tempted, He will show you a way out so that you will not give in to it."

1 Corinthians 10:13 (NLT)

Several friends were once eating dinner. Following a wonderful meal, the waiter presented the dessert options. Each person selected a favorite and soon each dessert was being delightfully consumed. Then a bizarre event occurred.

One of the women at the table picked up the pepper shaker and began sprinkling pepper all over her half-eaten piece of coconut cake. One by one, the other people at the table began to notice and observe. Chewing stopped and jaws dropped. Puzzled glances were exchanged. Obvious concerns were silently shared.

"What in the world is she doing? She's ruining a perfectly good piece of cake... Please tell me she's not going to eat that! How much pepper can one shaker hold?!?"

Finishing her task with a satisfied smile, she set the pepper shaker down and gently pushed the cake plate away. When her eyes met the worried stares of her tablemates, she simply proclaimed, "Oh... that's my method of behavior modification. I've eaten too much already!" You can imagine the immediate laughter and sighs of relief that followed!

Not a bad strategy. We wish we were strong enough to "just say no" all the time. But the truth is... sometimes we're not. Sometimes we have to do things that enable us to make the right choices. Things that lessen or remove the temptation. Things that guard against and save us from our weaknesses.

There are many different ways to "pepper a cake:"

    Change the locks

    Turn off the phone

Cut up the credit cards

Go to a meeting

Alter the normal route

Clean out the closet

Empty the refrigerator

Cancel a subscription

Log off the internet

Call a friend or sponsor

Sometimes God grants us the strength to simply say "no." Other times He provides us with the pepper.

Getting Noticed

"By this everyone will know that you are my disciples, if you have love for one another."

John 13:35 (NRSV)

The twenty-something-year-old young man got on the subway train with two of his friends. He was wearing multi-color plaid pants, a blue striped shirt, a light brown corduroy blazer (complete with the suede elbow patches), and orange Converse tennis shoes. His thick-rimmed black glasses added to the funky look he was apparently going for.

Even with all of that, the thing that stood out most about the guy was his hair. It was the reverse of a traditional mohawk. From his forehead to the back of his neck, his curly brown hair had a three-inch shaved strip. A typical mohawk cut would have gone along with his image. But the reverse mohawk made a more definitive statement.

Anytime someone takes a generally accepted idea and flips it on its end or reverses it, people take notice.

Jesus did it. He took traditionally accepted ideas and turned them upside-down. And He did it a lot.

> "Love your enemies." (*Matthew 6:44*)
>
> "If you try to keep your life for yourself, you will lose it. But if you give up your life for me, you will find true life." (*Matthew 16:25*)
>
> "Whoever wants to be a leader among you, must be your servant." (*Mark 10:43*)

Somehow we have tamed much of what Jesus said. We have made it socially acceptable to be a Christian, when in fact, Jesus' message was, and is, radically counter-cultural.

When we choose to live by Jesus' teachings, it's certain... people will stop and take notice.

The "Things We're Good At"

"So encourage each other and build each other up, just as you are already doing."

1 Thessalonians 5:11 (NLT)

The first grader hardly made it through the door before he proudly pulled his first report card from his backpack.

"Let's look at this!" he exclaimed.

Although a bit disappointed to find out that his report card didn't have A's, B's, and C's on it like he had heard about from his 5th grade friend, he listened as his dad read the list of skills along with his ratings. He didn't quite understand everything on it, but he smiled proudly as his parents told him what a great job he was doing in school. "I told you, I work hard there!" he stated emphatically.

Later at dinner, he glanced over toward the report card. "Hey Dad... Tell me again about the things I'm good at."

We all want to be encouraged. We want people to see and acknowledge the "things we're good at." We want to feel that what we have to offer is valuable. We want to know that what we do and have is enough.

There are plenty of places and people that beat us up and tear us down. That remind us of our shortcomings and failures. That make us feel inferior. The places and people that build us up and encourage us are often in short supply.

Maybe part of what it means to be a member of the family of faith is to find the time to remind one another once again "about the things we're good at."

Learn to Be Still

"You can be sure that God will take care of everything that you need."

Philippians 4:19 (The Message)

We've all heard the saying, "The grass is greener on the other side." The question is do we buy into it?

It's the "if-only" syndrome:

>If only I had a different job, I'd be happy.

>If only I were married to someone else, I'd be happy.

>If only I lived in a different city, I'd be happy.

>If only I had more money...

>If only I had a bigger house...

Later at dinner, he glanced over toward the report card. "Hey Dad... Tell me again about the things I'm good at."

We all want to be encouraged. We want people to see and acknowledge the "things we're good at." We want to feel that what we have to offer is valuable. We want to know that what we do and have is enough.

There are plenty of places and people that beat us up and tear us down. That remind us of our shortcomings and failures. That make us feel inferior. The places and people that build us up and encourage us are often in short supply.

Maybe part of what it means to be a member of the family of faith is to find the time to remind one another once again "about the things we're good at."

Learn to Be Still

"You can be sure that God will take care of everything that you need."

Philippians 4:19 (The Message)

We've all heard the saying, "The grass is greener on the other side." The question is do we buy into it?

It's the "if-only" syndrome:

>If only I had a different job, I'd be happy.

>If only I were married to someone else, I'd be happy.

>If only I lived in a different city, I'd be happy.

>If only I had more money...

>If only I had a bigger house...

> If only I had a better car...
>
> If only the kids were older...
>
> If only I could lose weight...

Some of us spend our lives chasing after greener grass, longing for things or people that we want to make a part of our own landscape. It's easy to become so focused on the search, the chase, the things we wish we had -- that we become blind to what is right in front of us.

The Eagles sing a song written by Don Henley and Stan Lynch called "Learn to Be Still:"

> Now the flowers in your garden
>
> They don't smell so sweet
>
> Maybe you've forgotten
>
> The heaven lying at your feet
>
> We keep asking
>
> How do I get out of here
>
> Where do I fit in
>
> Though the world is torn and shaken

Even if your heart is breakin'

It's waiting for you to awaken

And someday you will - Learn to be still.

The apostle Paul knew what it meant to be still:

"I've learned by now to be quite content whatever my circumstances. I'm just as happy with little as with much, with much as with little. I've found the recipe for being happy whether full or hungry, hands full or hands empty. Whatever I have, wherever I am, I can make it through anything in the One who makes me who I am." (*Philippians 4:11-13*, The Message).

In our seasons of discontent, may our eyes be opened to the blessings that we already enjoy. May our gratitude give us comfort, knowing that God will provide all that we need in His timing.

A Prayer of Thanksgiving

"Enter his gates with thanksgiving... For the Lord is good and his love endures forever."

Psalm 100: 4-5 (NIV)

O God, we thank you

...that when we don't know what words to pray,

You understand the language of our hearts.

...that when we don't know what moves to make,

You provide the direction for our steps.

...that when we don't know what to expect,

You give us the courage to trust.

...that when we don't know what we want,

You supply everything that we need.

...that when we don't know how to keep going,

You instill in us the strength to persevere.

...that when we don't know where we belong,

You remind us that we are members of Your family.

...that when we don't know where to turn,

You come running to us with open arms.

For all that we don't know, we thank You.

.....for it is through our unknowing,

that we come to know You more deeply

and once again find ourselves surrounded by Your love.

Snuggle Time!

"O Lord, you are a protecting rock of safety, where I am always welcome."

Psalm 71:3 (NLT)

Having just finished eating dinner, the young boy asked his mom, "Can you come snuggle on the couch with me?"

"Sure, let me clean up the kitchen first and then we'll do it."

After the dishes were done, she found him playing on the floor. "You wanna snuggle?"

He grabbed a blanket and jumped on the couch. "I've been waiting the whole day for this moment!"

They spent the next half-hour together, chatting about the day, feeling the breeze blow through the window, cheering on the Red Sox, talking about playing catch with dad in the front yard, being silly, and trying to figure out why friends aren't always friendly.

It was soon time for bed, and the party moved upstairs.

There is something wonderful about having someone's undivided attention and affection... it reminds us that we matter, that we count.

As followers of Christ, we have the privilege of spending that kind of time with God anytime. He longs for us to jump up into His arms and talk about the day, unload what we're worried about, and listen to how much we are loved.

The next time we find ourselves wanting a little snuggle-time, may we call out to the One who knows us best and loves us most. And remember, God has no dishes to finish... He's always available!

The Roller Coaster Life

"Let your unfailing love surround us, LORD, for our hope is in you alone."

Psalm 33:22 (NLT)

In October 2005, the Houston Astros were just one out away from playing in the World Series. Up by two runs, there was an air of celebration hanging over Minute Maid Park... the champagne was on ice, the ownership members were shifting from side to side, the fans held their breath, the dugout watched expectantly.

Then it happened.

St. Louis first-baseman Albert Pujols launched a towering, three-run homer to put the Cardinals on top. It was a devastating loss. Astros' catcher Brad Ausmus commented, "I don't ever celebrate before the last out is caught. Tonight is a good example of why I don't."

We've all heard it put another way. "Don't count your chickens before they hatch." But even when we follow that advice with our head, our heart doesn't always follow.

We know when we're getting close to realizing a dream. We know when what we've hoped for is just around the corner. We know when we're just about to be able to breathe a sigh of relief. And the hope-full part of us takes over. We get excited. We get happy. We wait expectantly.

Which is why it hurts so bad when the tide turns the other way. Or the home run ball gets launched. Or the deal falls through. Or the remission is over. Last-minute turn-of-events are always heartbreaking. Even when we tell ourselves not to celebrate too early, we just can't help looking forward. It seems to just be part of being human.

May we trust God to keep us steady, and to heal our hearts, on this roller-coaster life we live.

Light and Dark

"May the Lord bring you into an ever deeper understanding of the love of God and the endurance that comes from Christ."

2 Thessalonians 3:5 (NLT)

The check-out lines were three and four deep. As a new lane opened up, the mom wheeled her cart and her thirteen-month-old passenger in that direction. As her items were being scanned, the youngster smiled and babbled at the cashier. He grinned at the lady behind them. He waved and giggled when he realized he was at the center of attention.

"What a cutie pie!" the lady in line remarked. "I know," the cashier said, "he is a doll." His mom replied politely, then thought to herself, "You should have seen him ten minutes ago..."

He had been toddling around the store next to his mom for quite a while, when she decided it was time to get serious about attacking the shopping list. As she picked him up to put him in the cart, he began to protest. Strongly. And loudly.

Attempting to wrestle his way free, his mom finally got his feet through the leg holes and his bottom onto the seat. As she wheeled him off toward the cleaning supplies section, he continued to make lots of noise. Finally, realizing that his protests weren't changing anything, he resigned to his fate and turned it off. In no time, he was laughing at his mom making screeching noises as they went around the ends of the aisles.

We all have our great moments and our not-so-great moments. We are loving and generous one minute, and selfish and demanding the next. We might be quite a bit more subtle about it than our thirteen-month-old friend, but we are all mixtures of light and darkness. We each have the potential for greatness and the capability for destruction. It's who we are. And it's why we are all in need of salvation.

O God, thank you for saving us. And thank you that whether we find ourselves being cute and charming or loud and demanding, You are constant... loving us through it all.

Day-to-Day

"Give us today our daily bread."

Matthew 6:11 (NIV)

"Criminal Minds" is a television crime drama that revolves around an elite team of FBI profilers who analyze the country's most twisted criminal minds, trying to anticipate their next moves before they strike again. The task takes its toll on the personal lives of the team, albeit in various ways.

A couple of seasons back, one of the team members, Morgan, revealed a crisis of faith. We weren't told what it hinged on or when it all started, but his faith and belief in God had been shaken at best, possibly even shattered. Toward the end of one of the episodes, he found himself in a chapel… praying for the first time in years.

In the closing scene, Rossi – the most prominent member of the FBI unit and the only one privy to Morgan's struggle – confronts Morgan

"How's the faith thing going?"

Morgan looks at the ground, then back up at Rossi: "Day-to-day."

Isn't it that way for all of us? Crisis or no crisis... it's a day-to-day journey. There's no crystal ball to look into the future. God isn't asking us to trust him for next year, next month, or even next week. It's one day at a time. Trusting God to provide for *this* day. To meet our needs for *this* day. To give us the strength we need for *this* day.

This is the day that God made and has given to us. He can be trusted to see us through.

No Longer Condemned

"For God did not send his Son into the world to condemn the world,

but to save the world through him."

John 3:17 (NIV)

The 4th grader climbed into the car after his Math Club meeting, holding a piece of paper.

"Here's my contest results… Mr Regan said the team did pretty well."

"Great! How did *you* do?"

"I got half right, 15 out of 30." Then he added, "But Mr. Regan said that it's a pretty good score."

He pulled off his backpack and started buckling himself in. "It says that students who score 12 or more should be *condemned*. Wait, that's not it. They should be... oh, I don't know! Here. You can read it."

His mom took the paper and scanned the paragraph... "It says students who score 12 or more should be *commended*."

"What's that mean?"

"It means you should be praised. You should be told that you've done a good job."

"Whew. Oh, Cool!"

It's a wonderful feeling when we move from the world of being condemned to the ranks of the commended, isn't it? We think we're doomed to destruction only to find out that we're in line to receive praise.

God sent Jesus into the world, not to condemn us, but to save us. And we didn't even have to earn a good score on anything… Now that's grace!

The Oasis

"Clap your hands, all you peoples; shout to God with loud songs of joy."

Psalm 47:1 (NRS)

The Oasis. It is known as "The Sunset Capitol of Texas," a rambling restaurant with over 40 wooden decks nestled on a cliff overlooking Lake Travis in Austin. For locals and tourists alike, it is a favorite establishment.

One of the coolest traditions at the Oasis began over two decades ago, soon after it opened, and has continued through the years. Each night, when the sun finally settles into the horizon, a bell rings and those gathered on the many decks of The Oasis -- whether eating, drinking, dancing, serving, or conversing -- stop and give the scene a standing ovation. It is always a beautiful moment.

There are moments that simply call for praise. A recognition of God's amazing creation. An acknowledgement of the gift of life.

We often tell God what we're thankful for. But even then, it's somehow still partly about us... what we've received, what we have, what we've experienced. How often do we simply tell God how awesome He is? How often do we tell God how incredible He is?

Sometimes we just need to stop and offer God our own version of a round of applause.

O God, our Creator, Savior, Sustainer, and Hope. Here's to You!

"God" Friends

"Dear friends, since God loved us that much, we surely ought to love each other. No one has ever seen God. But if we love each other, God lives in us,

and his love has been brought to full expression through us."

1 John 4:11-12 (NLT)

As the writer proofread the email, she caught the mistake. Instead of "good friend," she had typed "god friend." She smiled. It wasn't too far off base.

Most of us have a few good friends. But what about "God" friends?

Friends who are a reflection of God's love
    who believe in us,

who cheer for us

who encourage us to listen for God's voice

who hold us accountable

who cry with us and rejoice with us

who listen and talk about things that matter

who make time to be present

who challenge us to be courageous and daring

who refuse to accept our superficial answers

who are there with open arms to pick us up when we fall

who make us laugh

who cause us to want to follow Jesus

Friends and acquaintances are a dime a dozen. Good, close friends are precious and few. But "God" friends are rare.

For the "God" friends in our lives, we say thank you. And may we be God friends, too.

Time to Surrender

"How precious is your unfailing love, O God!

All humanity finds shelter in the shadow of your wings."

Psalm 36:7 (NLT)

He missed the day in baby school when they taught that newborns are supposed to sleep 16-18 hours a day. On a good day, he sleeps maybe a total of 10 or 12 hours. And that's even counting the 15-minute catnaps he catches throughout the day!

Even when he does fall asleep, he fights it every step of the way. Whether being rocked in the rocking chair, held in someone's arms on the couch, or experiencing the parent-bop-around-the-room trick, he has to go through a fussy phase before he lets go and falls asleep. Sometimes it's a few whimpering cries. Other times it's a full-fledged battle. His eyes will be almost closed, and he'll mount a very fussy (and sometimes loud!) protest. Sometimes, it's one round. Other times, it's multiple rounds. Eventually though, his final hurrah ends and he melts into shut-eye, as his body relaxes and surrenders to the rest he so desperately needs.

He's not unlike many of us. We often fight against the very thing we need. We struggle against the thing that will bring us rest. We resist giving into the unknown. We mount multiple protests. And yet God cradles us in his arms and holds us tightly, whispering love, singing to us softly, waiting patiently for us to surrender.

May we stop our struggling and surrender to the rest and peace that we can find only in the great, big, loving arms of God.

In Unexpected Ways

About three o'clock in the morning, Jesus came to them, walking on the water. When the disciples saw him, they screamed in terror, thinking he was a ghost. But Jesus spoke to them at once. "It's all right," he said. "I am here! Don't be afraid."

Matthew 14:25-27 (NLT)

In October of 2005, there was a media frenzy outside of Fenway Park. Negotiations were taking place between the Boston Red Sox ownership and the General Manager, Theo Epstein. Leaks had occurred all weekend as to whether the two had reached an agreement... they *had* reached a deal, they *hadn't* reached a deal, money *was* an issue, money *wasn't* an issue, etc.

Red Sox Nation eagerly awaited to find out if Boston's own wonder-boy, the young genius who brought home the World Series championship for the first time in 86 years, would lead the team into the 2006 season and beyond.

As television cameras and journalists jockeyed for position and breaking news, what they didn't know was that the meeting was over. Epstein had resigned, and left the building. Following the meeting, huddled in Epstein's office were staff members trying to figure out how to get Epstein out of Fenway and home without being mauled by the media. Being Halloween, someone had a gorilla costume on hand. So in the middle of all of the hullabaloo, Epstein had strolled out of Fenway Park – in a gorilla suit – completely unnoticed.

Halloween Day 2005 at Fenway Park proved to us that it's possible to miss the very thing we are looking for, simply because it looks different than we expect or because we're not paying close enough attention.

In Advent and other seasons of our lives, our times of watching and waiting and hoping and celebrating the coming of Christ, it is still possible to miss the very things we are looking for. We get locked into certain expectations. We get wrapped up in the busy-ness of the season. We limit the ways we expect Christ to enter our lives. We stop paying attention.

O God, may we not miss the things we are looking for and the things that You provide. May we welcome You into our lives each and every day, even in the unexpected ways.

Admission to Worship

"But if we confess our sins to him, he is faithful and just to forgive us

and to cleanse us from every wrong."

1 John 1:9 (NLT)

In a Sunday morning worship service not too long ago, the music minister stopped a song that had somehow gone awry. He turned to the congregation and announced (primarily to the soloists and instrumentalists), "Let's pick that back up again at 4... I'm not sure what happened."

Before the director could begin the count again, one of the soloists addressed the congregation, speaking boldly into her microphone. "*I* know what happened, I goofed!" Her candid response drew both laughter and applause from the people in attendance. "That's *exactly* what happened... I goofed!"

A few moments later, the song was back in full swing, and the congregation continued worshipping. However, the jury remained out on which was the greater call to worship... the song itself, or the woman's courage in admitting her mistake.

Part of what it means to belong to the body of Christ is learning to admit when we are wrong. Another part of it is learning to not condemn. What happened in that particular worship service was a collision of both… and it led to worship.

May God give us the courage to admit our mistakes, and the grace to forgive.

Yesterday and Today

"This is the day the LORD has made. Let us rejoice and be glad in it."

Psalm 118:24 (NLT)

The first episode of "8 Simple Rules" after John Ritter's death was powerful. The hour-long special began with the Hennessy family learning of the unexpected death of Paul (Ritter's character), and followed Cate and the kids as they struggled to deal with the loss in their own ways. To help console the family, Cate's parents put aside their marital differences and came to be with the family in their time of need.

Soon after arriving, Cate's mother and father were arguing over sugar substitutes and who would get them out of the kitchen. Finally Cate's mother stopped and confessed how trivial they were being. She acknowledged Cate's pain, then volunteered to get the stuff herself. As she walked away, she addressed Cate, "Honey, can I get you something?"

Cate paused for a moment, then spoke. "Yeah. Get me yesterday."

How many of us, if granted a request, would join Cate in saying the same thing? "Get me yesterday..." When the one we loved was still here. When the kids were little. When life was a little less complicated.

"Get me yesterday..." When harmful words were unspoken. When poor choices were unmade. When opportunities had not yet been missed.

The truth is, while we may long for yesterday or yearn for tomorrow, today is what matters. Frederick Buechner writes of "today" in <u>Whistling in the Dark</u>:

> If you were aware how precious it is, you could hardly live through it. Unless you are aware of how precious it is, you can hardly be said to be living at all... All other days have either disappeared into darkness and oblivion or not yet emerged from them. Today is the only day there is.

God has given each of us the gift of today. May we choose to live it in His love and grace.

The "Stretching" Question

"Now we see things imperfectly as in a poor mirror, but then we will see everything with perfect clarity. All that I know now is partial and incomplete, but then I will know everything completely, just as God knows me now."

1 Corinthians 13:12 (NLT)

A young boy and his parents were watching a practice session of the New England Patriots training camp. After a few warm-up drills, the football players lined the field to do stretching exercises... "the boring part," as labeled by the youngster.

While the athletes conducted their regimen, the young boy let out a long sigh. "Why do they have to do this?" he asked. "They are stretching out their muscles and warming up their bodies," one of his parents responded. "It helps to keep them from getting hurt."

He sat thoughtfully for a minute, then spoke. "But what about Drew Bledsoe? Didn't he do these? And he still got hurt." Good question... Two years prior, Bledsoe had taken a hit in a ball game that not only caused a very serious injury, but also cost him his starting quarterback job.

Underneath the trappings of stretching and football, the youngster posed a deeper question that we all wrestle with:

> "Why does bad stuff happen to us even when we do all the right things and take all the necessary precautions?"

It's a question that no parent, scholar, theologian, or friend has ever been able to really answer. Life hands us things sometimes that just don't make sense. We minimize the risk factors, and yet disease descends. We follow the corporate policy, and yet our co-worker gets the promotion. We love and discipline our children, and yet they make poor choices. We put our heart into it, and yet it comes back broken.

There are things that happen for which we will never know the reasons and answers... at least on this side of eternity. Until then, may we have the courage to keep doing the right things. And to trust The One who knows us completely and loves us beyond our wildest dreams.

Reliving Mistakes

"If we confess our sins to him, he is faithful and just to forgive us

and to cleanse us from every wrong."

1 John 1:9 (NLT)

A Few Good Men. The storyline has military lawyer Daniel Kaffee (Tom Cruise) defending Marines accused of murder; they contend they were acting under orders of their imperious commanding officer.

There is a courtroom scene where Kaffee's assisting attorney, Jo Galloway (Demi Moore), goes way overboard in trying to convince the judge regarding the merit of an objection. Her actions make the defense look both foolish and desperate.

As soon as the court is recessed, Lieutenant Sam Weinberg (Kevin Pollak), the third member of the defense team, begins to berate Galloway for her actions. Kaffee interrupts. "Sam! She made a *mistake*... let's not relive it."

Good words for all of us to hear.

How many times do we find ourselves reliving a past mistake? We replay it in our mind, over and over, as if we are hoping for a different outcome. Or we kick ourselves again and again, because we can't believe we were capable of such a thing.

Reliving mistakes is a dangerous game. And it's an easy cycle to get stuck in. Before we know it, we are missing out on all that today has to offer because we're living in the past.

God's forgiveness is complete, hopeful, freeing, and life-giving. Today, may we stop reliving our past mistakes by owning up to our shortcomings, learning what we can from our experiences, and moving forward.

Even If

Without wavering, let us hold tightly to the hope we say we have,

for God can be trusted to keep his promise.

Hebrews 10:23 (NLT)

It was time to do homework, but the first-grader was far more interested in finishing the puzzle on the floor.

"Can I work on my puzzle after I finish my homework?"

"We'll see," his mom replied. "It depends on if there is time enough before your bath."

"I hope the answer is yes! If the answer is yes, then you're the greatest mother in the world!" Then he paused. "But if the answer is no... well... then you're still the greatest mother in the world!"

How many of us can say that we approach our requests to God with the same attitude? "This is what I want, what I hope for, what I'm praying for. But even if it doesn't work out my way, You are still an awesome God."

Shadrach, Meshach, and Abednego showed us that kind of approach. When King Nebuchadnezzar was sentencing them to the fiery furnace for refusing to worship a golden statue, they replied:

> If we are thrown into the blazing furnace, the God whom we serve is able to save us. He will rescue us from your power, Your Majesty. But even if he doesn't, Your Majesty can be sure that we will never serve your gods or worship the gold statue you have set up."
> *(Daniel 3:17-18)*

Even if He doesn't… Even if we don't get what I pray for… Even if it doesn't turn out like we want it to… we're still going to trust God and worship Him. Even if.

For All People

"May you have the power to understand, how wide, how long, how high,

and how deep His love really is."

Ephesians 3:18 (NLT)

He was the Guidance Department Director at a large high school in New England, when the powers-that-be strongly suggested that he gear his workload and focus toward collegiate preparation. He responded that his commitment was helping and working with all of the students, not merely those who were vying to get into Harvard and Yale.

As a result, his responsibilities were modified. Although he is no longer the director of the program, he continues to lead and guide and be a friend to high school students. And the kids on his campus know that he cares about them as individuals, regardless of their issues or challenges, goals or dreams.

The powers-that-be in Jesus' day offered similar advice: Spend your time with the up-and-comers, the religious leaders, those who have a handle on their lives. Don't waste your time on the losers and less fortunate.

But Jesus refused to draw lines. He welcomed the children. He crossed racial barriers. He ignored societal distinctions. He upended religious rules. Regardless of a person's story, He loved them. And they knew it.

We have established so many lines of distinction. Who's in and who's out. Who's hot and who's not. Who we accept and who we reject. Who's good enough and who's a loser. But God's love knows no labels. Everyone is important. Everyone is loved.

May we live our lives today as a reflection of God's love... for all people.

Push and Pull

"God saved you by his special favor when you believed.

And you can't take credit for this; it is a gift from God."

Ephesians 2:9 (NLT)

Sometimes he can do it alone. Other times he asks for help. But in the 16-month-old's world, anything 24-inches-and-under is game for climbing on. Chairs, couches, bookshelves, ottomans, beds, coffee tables, laundry baskets... the options are endless.

Chairs and couches are especially enticing when occupied by his 9-year-old brother. The times when he is able to get all the way up without help, his very next move is to push, pull, or drag his brother off, so that he can become the sole occupant. Then he sits back reigning proudly, grinning from ear to ear.

Other times, he will get stuck half-way up and begin to grunt or ask for help. His brother will reach down and give the toddler a boost, all-the-while knowing the chances are good that he himself will soon get the boot. It's an act of grace, simply because he loves his little brother.

It's an exercise that we often play out in our relationship with God. We need help or we get stuck or there's something that we want. We grunt, ask, and beg God for assistance. Yet as soon as we get where we want to go, we often push God back out of the equation. Then we sit proudly, wanting to believe we are independent and self-sufficient.

God loves us. And He is a God of grace. He answers our calls for help, knowing full well that chances are good we will abandon our need for him as soon as we get where we want to go.

Maybe one day, the toddler will realize it's more fun to sit next to his brother in the chair than it is to push him out. Maybe one day we too, will realize it's better to claim our dependence on God than to go it alone.

We are all humans in need of a savior. May we remember, acknowledge, and cling to the One who saves us and loves us completely.

These Days

"This is the day the LORD has made; let us rejoice and be glad in it."

Psalm 118:24 (NIV)

How many times have we heard, "I can't wait to graduate, so I can go to college!" Or "I can't wait to graduate college, so I can get a real job!" And those of us who have been-there-done-that think to ourselves "Enjoy these days while you can."

Yet we, too, do the same thing. We often live in anticipation of what is to come.

    As soon as the school year is over...

    As soon as I get married...

    As soon as I pay off the credit cards...

    As soon as we have kids...

As soon as I get a promotion...

As soon as the kids are grown...

As soon as I am retired...

And it happens even on a daily basis:

I can't wait for the bell to ring.

I can't wait for lunch.

I can't wait for naptime to be here.

I can't wait for it to be 5 o'clock.

I can't wait for him/her to get here.

I can't wait to go to sleep.

We would do well to heed our own advice, "Enjoy these days while we can."

Every day, every moment, is a precious gift. To live in constant anticipation of what has yet to be only robs us of the present. If we are not awake to the moments we are living, we might miss the blessings that God has for us in the here and now.

Even in the most frustrating of circumstances and in the most boring of times, there are magical moments of miracles if we only have eyes and ears to see and hear. It is in those moments that we are most aware and amazed by the incredible love and creativity of our Maker.

O God, give us the grace to live in the now. May we see the evidence of you and your love in the everyday moments of our lives. Amen.

An Evening Prayer for Those We Love

May God give you comfort

the feeling of His arms gently surrounding you

the warmth of His breath on your life

    May God give you peace

    the presence of a quiet calm

    the absence of fear and alarm

May God give you rest

the ability to sleep soundly and securely

the sustenance to continue to grow and learn

    And may you awake once again to an awareness

    of the Love that will never let you go. Amen.

Treasures Among the Trash

"Now glory be to God! By his mighty power at work within us, He is able to accomplish infinitely more than we would ever dare to ask or hope."

Ephesians 3:20 (NLT)

A handful of people stood at the corner waiting on the bus. Among them was an man who looked to be in his 60's. He was wearing a Harley t-shirt and jeans, holding a newspaper and backpack. Talking to no one in particular, he began:

> It started with a promise I made 21 years ago, and I've been doing it ever since. Why just yesterday I found a medical health CD for the computer. Somebody didn't want it, I guess, but the residents at the nursing home are really enjoying using it... Yeah, it's amazing the things I find that people have thrown away. I call them "treasures among the trash."

Apparently this man spends his days rummaging through garbage dumpsters, salvaging things and finding places where they are needed or can be used. It's not a bad way to spend one's life.

There are often a lot of experiences in our lives that we would like to throw away. We believe them to be useless or shameful. They cause us to feel worn out or broken. So we toss them out or bury them, hoping to never see them or be reminded of them again.

One of the amazing things about God is that He is in the business of finding treasures among our trash. When we offer the broken pieces of our lives to God, He is able to bring good out of even our smelliest trash. Sometimes the treasure may benefit us, making us stronger or wiser. Other times, it may benefit someone else.

Let's not bury or throw away the painful and embarrassing experiences in our lives. Instead may we offer all that we are to God... and trust that He will find the treasures among the trash.

Trusting the Process

"I am confident of this, that God who began a good work among you

will bring it to completion by the day of Jesus Christ."

Philippians 1:6 (NLT)

For his ninth birthday, the young boy asked for contacts. Since he had proven to be ultra-responsible with his glasses, and he played whatever sport was in season, his parents said yes.

When the doctor's assistant first instructed him on how to put them in and take them out, it took him a solid 30 minutes to do it. His motivation to wear them outweighed his frustration and discouragement, but he would occasionally comment about how difficult it was to do. His mom reassured him that it would get easier each time, that one day he would pop them in and out without even thinking about it.

Two weeks into contact life, putting in his lenses was only a three or four minute process. Taking them out was piece of cake. At that point, he said to his mom, "I know you told me it would get easier, but I didn't see how... Now I know you were right!" A few weeks later, it was all smooth sailing.

Sometimes we just have to trust the process.

Rehab after an injury or surgery. Learning a new skill or trade. Training for an athletic event. Grieving a deep loss. Staying sober. Rebuilding a relationship. Going on a diet. It's easy to get discouraged in the early days, wondering if anything will ever be different, questioning if it is worth it, doubting that we can stay with it.

Sometimes we just have to trust the process.

We take it one day at a time, focus on what we can do, and concentrate on what is in front of us for that moment. We might not understand how, but we press on, believing that it may or may not get easier, but it will get better. One day, we'll look back and see our progress. We'll reach our goal, get our chip, reap the benefits, learn to smile again.

As long as we just trust the process.

Leaves

"For everything there is a season, and a time for every matter under heaven."

Ecclesiastes 3:1 (NRS)

He loves leaves. In fact, he has a favorite tree.

When his family used to take him for stroller rides around the neighborhood, he would begin ooh-ing and aah-ing and pointing at a particular tree as soon as they rounded the corner. As they approached the tree, they would stop so that he could touch the leaves. Now that he's found his legs, he toddles down the sidewalk and around the corner. But it's still the same routine. The stop by the tree is mandatory.

His first trip to the tree after the leaves began falling left him puzzled. He looked at the leaves on the tree. He looked at the leaves on the ground. He looked at his mom. Then he reached down and picked up a leaf. He gave it to his mom, took her hand, and guided it to one of the lower hanging branches. He repeated this as long as his mom would cooperate. In his thirteen-month-old way, he was trying to put the leaves back on the tree.

In our own ways, we often try to put the leaves back on the tree.

Just as a toddler cannot understand that leaves drop off during the fall but grow back in the spring, the seasons of life often leave us puzzled. We want things to stay the same. Or, we long for things to be as they were before. We make all sorts of attempts to put the leaves back on the branches.

But we're old enough to know that life doesn't work that way. As much as we sometimes wish it did, there are things that we cannot change. There are things that cannot be undone. There are things that cannot be replaced. There are losses that we simply must live with.

The next time we find ourselves trying to put the leaves back on the tree, may we remember and trust that the One who created us and gave us life, is also the One who sustains us through all of its seasons.

Stripes

"May the God who gives endurance and encouragement give you a spirit of unity among yourselves as you follow Christ Jesus."

Romans 15:5 (NIV)

In *Racing Stripes*, a comical family movie in which the animals talk, Stripes is a young zebra who gets left behind by a traveling circus. The man who finds him owns a farm next to a Kentucky race track. As Stripes grows up, he watches the race horses train and run, and develops his own dreams of racing. He loves to run. And he's fast.

One day at the border fence, two adolescent thoroughbreds are teasing Stripes. The father of one of the thoroughbreds with championship bloodlines comes over and reprimands the boys for associating with such an animal. As they trot away, Stripes asks Tucker, his barnyard Shetland-pony-friend, "Why doesn't their dad want them talking to me?"

"Because you're different. And to some horses, different is scary."

Tucker is right. And different is scary not only to horses. Different is often scary to us. We're often afraid of what is unfamiliar. We are leery of what we don't know.

We often distance ourselves from people who are different from us. Be it skin color or race, religion or politics, schools or sports, ability or challenge, economics or education. We tend to draw lines to keep "them" out and to keep "us" in.

It's amazing what happens when we are willing to cross those lines and get to know someone who falls into our category of being "different." The stereotypes fade. The labels lift. The walls tumble.

We are not expected to like everyone we meet or know. But chances are that when we take the time to get to know someone, we find they are not all that different after all. For the most part, we all have the same fears, hopes, worries, and dreams. We all want to matter. And we all want to be loved.

May God calm the fear that causes us to exclude people simply because they are different, so that we may reach out to others with grace and love and understanding.

Stripes, Part 2

"Cast all your anxiety on him, because he cares for you."

1 Peter 5:7 (NRS)

Same movie – *Racing Stripes*. Later in the film, Stripes begins training to race. His owner, who had previously trained champion steeds and was known as "Chief" to the barnyard animals, had agreed to the task. They plowed a track in the corn field and Stripes had gone to work. He was breaking record times around the track, but having trouble with the gate. Every time he got near the starting gate, he would get spooked and freak out.

In a conversation with Tucker (his Shetland pony veteran trainer-friend), Stripes expressed concern about his ability to compete. "I know I can run," he said, "but I'm worried about the gate."

Tucker promptly responded, "You keep running. Don't worry about the gate. Leave that to Chief... he knows what he's doing."

We all have our own "gate anxieties," don't we? Those things that seem to throw us off balance. Things that freak us out. Things that we just can't seem to conquer. Things that seem to hold us back from becoming great. Things we're worried about ever gaining the ability to overcome. Things we're simply just… afraid of.

Maybe we would do well to listen to Tucker's advice. Focus on what we can do, and let God worry about our "gates." We can trust that He will help us learn and deal with those things that spook and worry us.

Imitators All

"Therefore be imitators of God... and live in love, as Christ loved us."

Ephesians 5:1-2 (NRS)

They were looking out the window, watching the snow fall... Mom on her knees, and the toddler standing atop a wooden Sesame Street activity cube beside her. He was laughing at the way the glass would fog with his breath, then wildly wiping it clean with his palms.

His mom, amazed at his energy and wonder, sighed, folded her arms on the sill, and rested her chin on top. The toddler paused and examined her posture. Then he proceeded to place his arms on the sill, too. After one more glance to make sure he had it right, he rested his chin on his arms, smiling at his accomplishment.

He's an imitator. It's the way he learns. It's the way he grows.

We, too, are imitators. We borrow words and phrases and craft them into our own. We see styles that we like and we adopt them for ourselves. We watch others perform and advance and make mental notes in our files. We copy the behaviors of those we admire.

We are imitators. It's the way we learn. It's the way we grow.

"Be imitators of God," Paul says. In Jesus Christ, we have seen God in human form. May we learn and grow in the love that Jesus demonstrated and lived each and every moment.

Receiving Love

"Meanwhile, Jesus was in Bethany at the home of Simon, a man who had leprosy. During supper, a woman came in with a beautiful jar of expensive perfume. She broke the seal and poured the perfume over his head."

Mark 14:3 (NRS)

Mark tells us a story that happened on Tuesday of what we have come to call Holy Week. It was two days before Passover. Two days before Jesus would be betrayed. Quite a few people were at Simon's house. We can imagine what the conversations must have been about... the amazing entrance into the city just two days earlier, the events at the Temple the day before. We can only imagine how heavy Jesus' heart must have been in anticipation of the days ahead.

So everyone is gathered. And while Jesus is eating supper, a woman comes into the room, breaks open the seal on a beautiful jar of perfume, and pours it over his head. It may seem strange to us in our modern culture, but in those days it was an extravagant act of love. Mark tells us that some in the room grew angry, righteously angry. But he also leaves room for others present to have possibly appreciated the moment for what it was.

Perhaps one of the most interesting things about what transpired in that house just outside of Jerusalem and just outside of the passion to come, is that Jesus allowed himself to be loved. God's Son, the Giver of Life, Love Incarnate... placed himself in a position to receive love.

We talk so much about loving others. We encourage each another to commit acts of love. We know that others will recognize us as followers of Christ by the way we love one another. But sometimes we get so focused on giving love, that we forget that it's okay to receive love, too.

As Jesus approached what had to be the most difficult of days, he leaned into the love that was given him. By this woman. By his disciples. By his friends. We can face our own tough times the same way, by allowing those around us, to love us.

Don Henley and Glenn Frey of the Eagles wrote:

> Desperado, why don't you come to your senses?

Come down from your fences, open the gate

It may be rainin', but there's a rainbow above you You

better let somebody love you, before it's too late.

In these often-difficult days, may we be open to receive love from those God has placed in our lives.

Who's Cool?

"There is no longer Jew or Greek, there is no longer slave or free, there is no longer male and female; for all of you are one in Christ Jesus."

Galatians 3:28 (NRS)

A second-grader was educating his parents on the ways of the K-2 school bus world: "There are four kinds of kids on the bus," he explained. "Dorkies, wimpies, mediums, and cool."

His parents smiled at one another. "Who determines who is what?"

"Well," he continued. "The dorkies and wimpies are mostly kindergarten and 1st graders. The mediums are 2nd graders... with some 1st graders mixed in. But the cool kids are *definitely* second grade kids."

"So which one are you?" his mom asked.

He grinned. "Right now I'm a medium kid... but I'm working my way up to being cool."

No matter what age we are, we all have ways of defining who's in and who's out. From lunch tables and locker rooms to workplaces and neighborhoods, we seek to establish lines of demarcation.

James and John attempted to do it when they asked Jesus if He would reserve them seats of honor on either side of Him. Mark (Chapter 10) tells us that the other disciples were "indignant" when they overheard the brothers' request. Chances are, their anger may have been as much about jealousy as it was about righteousness.

The truth is that we all want to belong. We all want to be included. We want to know that we are accepted. We want to be – for lack of a better term – *cool*.

Here is the good news: In the Kingdom of God, all are included. No one gets left out. Everyone is in. We don't get to say who sits in the back of the bus or who is the most important in the company. In the economy of God, everyone matters and everyone counts.

Breathe

"He himself gives life and breath to everything, and he satisfies every need there is."

Acts 17:25 (NLT)

There are times when we feel trapped. We feel locked in to where we are... personally, professionally, geographically, financially, physically, etc. There are bills to pay, obligations to fulfill, people to care for, expectations to meet. There often seems to be no escape and no relief.

Twenty-something singer-songwriter Anna Nalick seems to capture that feeling in her song, "Breathe (2AM)." The verses illustrate a young woman ending a relationship, a young man addicted to alcohol, and a writer struggling between transparency and secrecy. Then the chorus:

> Cause you can't jump the track, we're like cars on a cable,

And life's like an hourglass, glued to the table.

No one can find the rewind button girl (boy),

So cradle your head in your hands.

And breathe, just breathe,

Whoa breathe, just breathe.

Anna once commented regarding the song, "I wrote 'Breathe' intending to remind myself to accept what I couldn't change and look for a brighter future in my lessons learned."

Breathe. Just breathe.

We read in Genesis that God breathed life into man (2:7). Mark tells us that when Jesus healed the deaf man (7:34), he looked toward heaven, took a deep breath, spoke the words "Be opened," and at once the man could hear. In John's post-resurrection account (20:22), Jesus spoke peace to his disciples, breathed on them, and gave them the Holy Spirit.

Breath is the very sustenance of our lives. Without it, we die.

Whether we find ourselves feeling trapped or feeling full of life, may we stop long enough to just breathe, listening to the air flow in and out of our body... and may our breathing remind us, that the God who created us also sustains us and heals us at every turn of our lives.

Breathe. Just breathe.

Credit Who?

"Take care! Don't do your good deeds publicly, to be admired, because then you will lose the reward from your Father in heaven."

Matthew 6:1 (NLT)

At his Inaugural Luncheon in January of 1985, President Ronald Reagan informed the guests that he kept a plaque on his desk with a quote that reflected what he firmly believed. It read:

There is no limit to what man can accomplish if he doesn't care who gets the credit.

Reagan was onto something. We have become a credit-hungry society. We want others to recognize the things we do. We want to make sure that we get credited with our latest good idea. We want to make sure that someone notices when we do something helpful for someone. We want to get proper credit for our words, deeds, and actions. However, our hunger for recognition and attention often gets in the way of accomplishing and achieving things for the greater good.

How many great movements have been thwarted because potential leaders got into a power struggle? How many families have been divided because one member didn't get the recognition they thought they deserved? How many churches have split because one faction didn't feel enough attention was being paid to their own cause or mission? How many limits do we put on what we can accomplish because we are too caught up in making sure we get credited for our role?

The answer is "too." Too many.

Maybe it's time we remind ourselves that it's not all about us. Whether we ever will get credit or not, should not drive what we choose to do. Whether we will ever receive recognition or thanks, should not deter us from doing the right thing. God has called us to love one another. May we focus on living and loving... and leave the credit- and reward-giving up to God.

It just might amaze us what great things we can accomplish!

Pleasure and Pain

"And now may God, who gives us his peace, be with you all. Amen."

Romans 15:33 (NLT)

He toddle-ran across the family room after spotting his blankie in the corner. Just before he got there, he tripped and fell. Hard. Usually one to catch himself with his hands, this time the 16-month-old caught his forehead on his Fisher-Price holiday train instead.

He jumped up into his mom's arms and cried for a couple of minutes. Then, sporting his own version of holiday colors on his head, he side-stepped the train and went about his business.

The train, the very thing that had been bringing him so much pleasure, suddenly caused him pain.

Holidays can be like that. There is so much talk about celebration and joy and happiness. Yet the very things that bring many of us pleasure can also bring many of us pain. We miss those we love. We battle depression. We long to find that special someone. We struggle with family relationships. We hope time passes quickly and ushers us into a new year. For some reason, the holidays seem to magnify whatever emotions we are dealing with... both good and bad.

In the midst of our celebrating the birth of Christ, may we not forget that there are those around us who are hurting. And in the midst of our pain, may we not forget that the One who is celebrated is also the One who gives us hope in the midst of our pain.

When the Lights Go Down

For God has not given us a spirit of fear and timidity, but of power, love, and self-discipline.

2 Timothy 1:7 (NLT)

Faith Hill sings a song called "When the Lights Go Down" (written by Craig Wiseman, Jeffrey Steele, and Rivers Rutherford). The first verse paints a picture of a bartender at closing time – cleaning up, counting tips, and wrestling the temptation to pour himself a drink. The second verse is about a once-famous movie star trying unsuccessfully to contact her friends – who departed quickly when the fame and flash disappeared. Then comes the chorus:

> When the lights go down
>
> And there's nothing left to be
>
> When the lights go down
>
> And the truth is all you see

> When you feel that hole inside your soul
>
> And wonder what you're made of
>
> Well, we all find out
>
> When the lights go down

There comes a time in each of our lives when the lights go down. It may be as simple as the end of another day. It may a job change or a move. It may be the loss of a relationship or the death of a loved one. It may be an intentional look into the depth of our souls.

However it comes, when the lights go down we find ourselves face to face with the truth of who we really are... the masks are off, the charades are stopped, and no one else is watching. It is a sobering moment of truth, which can cause us to ask questions such as the one found later in the song:

> And I wonder if all my life's about / The sum of all my fears and all my doubts

As children of God, our lives are not defined by our fears and our doubts, but rather by God's love. In the moments when the lights go down, may we not get scared or grow discouraged, but may we listen to the voice of God telling us who we are and how much He loves us.

Words

*"So the Word became human and lived here on earth among us.
He was full of unfailing love and faithfulness."*
John 1:14 (NLT)

O God,

Sometimes we are at a loss for words
Like when someone we know is hurting
And we want to say something that will ease the pain
Yet we know that there is nothing we can say that will do that

Sometimes we are at a loss for words
Like when a project is due at school or at work
And we're staring at the blank paper or screen
Hoping for an "ah-ha" moment to get us jump-started
Wishing for time to slow down until the words start flowing

Sometimes we are at a loss for words

Like when we are trying to tell a friend what we really think and feel
And we don't want to hurt their feelings
Or cause distance or separation to come between us
Praying that what we say and how we say it will come across in love

Sometimes we are at a loss for words
Like when we are trying to tell You the deepest longings of our hearts
And we know that You already know what's inside
But we also know that trying to give words to what we feel can be helpful to us
But usually the tears and silence just take over

O God, You are the Word of Life
You spoke the world into existence
You spoke new life into Lazarus
You spoke healing to the sick
You spoke peace to your disciples
You spoke your Spirit into your followers
You are the Word of Life

Please speak your words to us now
Of creativity and of life
Of peace and of grace
Of courage and of love. Amen.

Everything We Need

"And my God will fully satisfy every need of yours according to his riches in glory in Christ Jesus."

Philippians 4:19 (NRS)

There was a young girl living in an adolescent residential treatment center whose 16th birthday fell in the middle of the chaos following the 9/11 terrorist strikes. Part of the response of this tough-as-nails kid to the tragedy, was to send all of the money she received for her birthday to the relief fund in New York.

An adult complimented and affirmed her decision saying, "That's a really great thing to do. But $200 is a lot of money... that's everything you had." "I know," said the girl, "but my parents have always been generous with me. They'll make sure I have whatever I need."

Wow. Here was a young girl, who under normal circumstances, probably would have spent her money on less-than-desirable items. Yet her compassion for the 9/11 victims, along with her belief that her parents would provide the necessary things for her, led her to send her money to New York instead.

Without even realizing it, this teenager painted a great picture for the rest of us of what it means to share what we have been given, trusting that God will continue to meet our needs.

May we give generously to those around us who are in need -- not just monetarily and materially, but also in the intangible ways -- and trust that God will continue to provide everything that we need.

The Basics

"Jesus said, "But even more blessed are all who hear the word of God and put it into practice."

Luke 11:28 (NLT)

The fall is that time of the year where we can find just about any professional sport we are looking for. Baseball season is nearing the playoffs; football season is underway; and hockey and basketball are entering pre-season routines. The ultimate goal for any and all of these competitors is to win the championship of their respective league.

If we look at those who become championship teams, the one thing they all have in common is that they have mastered the basics. They have learned and practiced the fundamental elements of the game. Hitting. Throwing. Catching. Fielding. Base running. Shooting. Dribbling. Passing. Blocking. Tackling. All the incredible offensive and defensive plays that we get to enjoy watching come from mastering the basics.

Some religious leaders of Jesus' day asked him to identify the most important commandment. Jesus' response was this:

> Love the Lord your God with all your heart, and with all your soul, and with all your mind. This is the greatest and first commandment. And a second is like it: You shall love your neighbor as yourself. (*Matthew 22:37-39*)

Jesus then explained that everything else hangs on these two commandments. In other words, these two commandments are fundamental. These are the basics. All the other stuff of the Christian life comes as a result of mastering these two commandments.

Want to be a champion? Want to be the best we can be as followers of Christ? Let's keep it simple. *Practice the basics.*

Passion, Anyone?

"I came that they may have life, and have it abundantly."

John 10:10 (NRSV)

Serendipity stars John Cusack as Jonathan, and Kate Beckinsale as Sara. The two meet by chance on one wonderful New York night and let fate decide if they should meet again to continue their attraction. Ten years later, they do. It's a predictable, yet warm and entertaining tale.

Jeremy Piven plays Dean, Jonathan's best friend and number one sidekick in trying to help him find Sara once again. Dean is a writer for the New York Times. An obituary writer, that is. At one point in the movie, he is both defending and questioning the necessity and dignity of his job. His last comment is piercing. "Long ago, the Greeks didn't even write obituaries. They only asked one question: Did he have passion?"

What a question!

Let's make it present tense... Do we have passion? *Why* do we do what we do? Are we passionate about life? What drives us and motivates us? Do we get up in the morning with a sense of purpose?

It's easy to lose our passion. The ordinariness of life can drain it. The trials of life can steal it. The demands of life can diminish it. However, without passion, life is reduced to simply being able to cross another day off of the calendar.

If we've lost our passion it's worth doing whatever it takes to go find it and get it back.

Once Upon a Time

"You both precede and follow me. You place your hand of blessing on my head. Such knowledge is too wonderful for me, too great for me to know!"

Psalm 139:5-6 (NLT)

Just one day shy of his 4th birthday, Stanton went to live with Jesus. His homegoing followed a courageous and inspirational fight against neuroblastoma. In his brief time on earth, he touched the lives of many people in amazing ways.

Stanton's mom maintained a website chronicling their journey, and she once posted the following story:

> Stanton had gotten very interested in Bible stories so I decided to get him a Hermie Bible so that we could read and he would understand. When he opened it, he was very verbal in the fact that this was not the kind of Bible he wanted. Well, Christmas morning

Santa brought him a Precious Moments Bible which is a real Bible with Precious Moment inserts. When he saw it he said, "This is the Bible me wanted." Well, Stanton knew several stories by heart and I loved to hear him tell them, so he got us all lined up sitting on the edge of the bed while he fixed his chair just right. He opened his new Bible and I was waiting on this great story of Jonah, Daniel, or Noah. I guess by now you have figured out that is not the story we got. He very seriously said, "Once upon a time, there were 3 little pigs..."

Even in his young years, Stanton seemed to know what we sometimes forget... that God is not only found in the stories of the Bible, He is also found in the stories of our lives.

All too often, we tend to compartmentalize our lives. God and religious stuff in one area, the rest of life in another. We go to church, pray, read the Bible, complete our checklist of things-we-should-do-to-be-a-good-Christian. And then we go on with the rest of our lives. All the time forgetting the basic truth: God *is in* the rest of our lives.

Storytelling is powerful stuff. May we take the time to tell one another stories from the pages of our lives, if only to help one another hear and see God among them together. Whether we experience the rebelliousness of Jonah or the courageousness of Daniel, the obedience of Noah or the fearfulness of the three little pigs, God is with us every step of the way.

Second-Guessing

"That evening, the disciples were meeting behind locked doors because they were afraid... Suddenly, Jesus was standing there among them! 'Peace be with you,' he said."

John 20:19 (NLT)

Michael was working as a U.S. Airways ticket agent in Portland, Maine, on September 11, 2001. He issued boarding passes to Mohamed Atta and Abdulaziz Alomari, two of the terrorists who would hijack a plane out of Boston later that morning. Once his interviews with the FBI were declassified, he spoke about his experience.

He says the faces of the hijackers and the day of the attacks continue to haunt him. He remembers being suspicious about the pair's expensive, first-class, one-way tickets to Los Angeles. He remembers Atta's angry face when he told them they would have to recheck in Boston. He confesses, "I said to myself, 'If this guy doesn't look like an Arab terrorist, then nothing does.' Then I gave myself a mental slap, because in this day and age, it's not nice to say things like this."

He says he has yet to fully come to grips with his brush with the terrorists. He wishes he would have acted on his suspicions. He still feels guilty and partly responsible for what happened that day. He continues to struggle with the questions of "Why didn't I...?" and "What if...?"

We can empathize with Michael, because we all know on some level what he is going through. The gnawing at the pit of our stomachs. The mind games that go on in our head. The longing for a chance to go back and rewrite the script. The guilt we feel when we believe we were responsible. The heavy, back-breaking weight of the "what if's?"

We all have things in our lives we wish we could do over. Times when our gut told us something and we didn't act on it. Times when we had a hunch, but ignored it. Times when our actions, or lack of them, led to things happening we wish we could change.

We each have different ways of dealing with the pain. In the hours and days following Jesus' betrayal and crucifixion, Judas hung himself. Peter cried and ran. Thomas went AWOL for a while. Most of his disciples scattered. Mary Magdalene and two other women remained loyal.

And then Jesus showed up. Offering peace. Offering forgiveness. Offering hope. Offering a love that would not let them go.

To Michael and to each of us, Jesus comes again and again... bringing peace, hope, healing, and love. May we have the courage to embrace Him and allow His love to heal us and make us whole.

Struggling to Learn

"But grow in the special favor and knowledge of our Lord and Savior Jesus Christ."

2 Peter 3:18 (NLT)

A baby lies on the floor, playing. He's mastered rolling over from his back to his tummy, but he's still practicing the tummy-to-back move. So sometimes he gets stuck. When that happens, he gets frustrated, drops his head onto his hands and cries.

He's also figuring out that he can scoot around if he makes the right moves, but he's not always sure what the right moves are. He reaches for a toy or a stuffed animal. If he can grab it, he's satisfied momentarily. If it's just out of reach, he gets frustrated, drops his head onto his hands and cries.

It's difficult for a parent not to want to rescue him. Roll him back onto his back. Move the toy within reach. Make the big bad frustration monster go away.

But babies don't develop skills by merely getting older. They have to have the chance to learn and grow. They have to have the chance to practice new skills. In other words, they have to struggle. Always getting rescued won't help him in the long run. On the other hand, always left in a puddle of frustration can leave him defeated.

Sometimes we wonder why God doesn't rescue us from our struggles. We wonder why he allows us to become frustrated, even feeling hopeless at times. We pray and cry and nothing changes. Other times, we ask God for help and it's obvious that he comes to our rescue. Maybe it's because God knows we need to struggle at times in order to learn and grow.

Far better than earthly parents, God always knows when to rescue and when to let us struggle. Because of His ultimate love for us, we can trust that He knows what He's doing. And God always parents us in love and with patience.

O God, help us to grow. And may we continue to feel your presence... even when we struggle. Amen.

Been There, Done That

"Praise be to the God and Father of our Lord Jesus Christ, the Father of compassion and the God of all comfort, who comforts us in all our troubles, so that we can comfort those in any trouble with the comfort we ourselves have received from God."

2 Corinthians 1:3-4 (NIV)

We've all heard the saying... "Been there, done that." Sometimes it's an expression of accomplishment. Other times it's an expression of dismissal. Still other times it is an expression of understanding or identification. We've even added some flavor to the comment on occasion. "Been there, done that, bought the T-shirt." Or "Been there, done that, don't want to go back."

At the risk of stating the obvious, here are some translations:

> I've traveled that road before.

> I know what it's like.

I've been through a similar experience.

I understand what you're going through.

I survived to tell about it!

There are some experiences that change our lives forever. Happenings that don't allow us to look at things the same anymore. Journeys that leave us with a deeper understanding of ourselves and others.

Encounters with the grace of God are like that. Anyone who has experienced true brokenness — who has come face to face with the reality of their desperate need for God's grace — cannot walk away unchanged. Whether grace is needed for strength to endure or for healing or forgiveness... when received, it changes us forever. Our *been there, done that's* become remarks of encouragement and hope and comfort and solidarity, rather than dismissal, condescension, or judgment. We understand the pain of another's brokenness. We are not so quick to judge another's choices. We identify with another's heartache.

This amazing grace of God is available to everyone. Pray that God will help us to use the "been there, done that" experiences of our lives to bring hope and healing and grace to the people we encounter along the way.

The Only Day

"Teach us to make the most of our time, so that we may grow in wisdom."

Psalm 90:12 (NLT)

In *Field of Dreams*, we were introduced to Archibald "Moonlight" Graham, a baseball player from the 1920's. Moonlight's dream was to play professional baseball in the major leagues. During the conclusion of one season, he was called up from the minors. In the final game, he got to play one-half inning in right field, but he never got to bat. Following that season, he retired from baseball and went to school to become a doctor.

In the movie, Ray Kinsella (Kevin Costner) asks Moonlight what that experience was like. He responds:

> "It's like you get this close to your dreams and then watch them brush past you like a stranger in the crowd. At the time you don't think much of it. You know, we just don't

recognize the most significant moments of our lives while they are happening... back then I thought, "Well, there'll be other days." I didn't realize that was the *only* day."

There's something about our lives that lulls us into believing that there will always "be other days." We go to bed each night, assuming we will awake to another day. We take things for granted, assuming we will always have them. We undervalue our relationships, assuming they will always be there. We often miss some of life's greatest blessings because of our "there will be other days" mentality.

When is the last time we...

...stopped to watch the sunset?

...listened to a toddler giggle?

...went to feed the ducks?

...told someone we loved them?

...laughed so hard our stomach hurt?

...smelled fresh flowers?

...cried when we watched the news?

...launched a kite on a windy day?

...bought ourselves a present?

...walked outside to take a deep breath of fresh air?

...thanked God for the day?

Our challenge is to live fully alive, to be awake to the present. May we go forth and live this day as if it were *the only day*!

Blankie

"I'll never let you down, never walk off and leave you."

Hebrews 13:5 (The Message)

The preschooler and his mom were pulling into the parking lot when they realized that "Blankie" had gotten left at home. "Blankie," a 12-inch, fairly square, one-side-satin, one-side-flannel, blue blanket, had been with the little boy from his beginning and still generally went everywhere with him. The general routine was that Blankie would go in the backpack when the little boy met his teacher at the door. So since they were at the school and it was time to start his mom assured him that he would be fine and she would bring it when she picked him up.

What she knew, was that he didn't see or touch Blankie while he was in the classroom. What she realized later, is *that* was not what mattered. It was simply *knowing* Blankie was in his backpack that provided him with security and comfort at school. He didn't have to see it or touch it. It was Blankie's *presence* that he counted on.

Blankie has had perfect attendance since.

So we're all grown up and way past preschool days... and our "blankies" have changed. But *presence* is still the key, especially to those of us who lean on God for our comfort and security. For while we can't see or touch God, he is never absent. He has promised to never leave us. We can always count on his presence to comfort and sustain us.

Snow Farms

Then Jesus said, "Come to me, all of you who are weary

and carry heavy burdens, and I will give you rest."

Matthew 11:28 (NLT)

The blizzards that occasionally hit the Northeast can leave Boston and its surrounding towns covered in over two to three feet of snow. Road crews and public works departments everywhere work around the clock to get the region back up and functioning.

In the streets of Boston, there is no room to merely push the snow aside. There's no place to pile it on a corner. There's no space to plow it into mounds. The streets are too narrow. The buildings and houses are too close. So what is a city to do with literally hundreds of tons of snow?

They truck it to "snow farms" – designated plots of land where large amounts of snow can be safely dumped and piled after being removed from the city streets. These snow farms are distant from wells, rivers, and wetlands, so that the contaminated plowed snow doesn't harm wildlife or ruin water supplies. Without these designated snow farms, the city would be locked down for days, sometimes weeks.

The blizzards of our personal lives often leave behind snow that must be dealt with. Baggage, emotions, wounds, questions... things that demand our attention if we are to continue about our lives. Sometimes we simply try to push it aside, or shovel it into a pile. Sometimes we try to plow through it to keep moving forward. Sometimes it works. Other times, there is simply too much hurt, too much carnage, to just let it sit and wait for it to melt. We have to find a safe place to dump it.

We all need to have our own snow farms. Places where we can go when things pile up too high. People we can trust to tell when there's no room to move forward. Times when we can unload whatever is bothering us. Regardless of what our snow farms may look like... friends, therapists, quiet times, stress-relieving activities, meetings, journaling, etc… may we always remember that Jesus stands ready and waiting to handle all the snow we care to unload.

O God, today may we take refuge in you, our ultimate Snow Farm.

Circle Up

"For we know that when this earthly tent we live in is taken down – when we die and leave these bodies – we will have a home in heaven."

2 Corinthians 5:1 (NLT)

One of the things that always seems to show up in newspapers and television shows at year's end are lists of people who died during that year. "People We Said Good-Bye to in 2008." From celebrities and movie stars to leaders and peacemakers. The list is always quite long. It's sort of sobering to read through such commentaries.

Then we can add our own losses to the list. Losses that would never make a national list, but nevertheless whose absence is felt deeply in our own lives.

We never stop missing those we love, do we? Be it two days, six months, or twenty-nine years since they left us... there's always a longing to see them again. Time helps to heal the acuteness of our pain; but, well, we still miss them.

Chris Rice sings a song called "Circle Up" that includes these lyrics:

> Hear the hum of angel curiosity
>
> The children of the Lord are gathering
>
> Finally the day we've all been dreaming of
>
> Called up forever in his love
>
> Circle up, circle up around the throne
>
> Old and young, saints of every history
>
> Great and small, angels all and seraphim
>
> Grab a hand, twirl a dance, circle up and worship Him

There will be a day when we will be reunited with those we love. And along with those from every era of history, every walk of life, every nation and tribe, and every corner of heaven... we will all join together to worship the God who loves us and calls us his own.

Jump Practice

"For I can do everything with the help of Christ who gives me the strength I need."

Philippians 4:13 (NLT)

A young army lieutenant discussed jumping for precision. Out of airplanes!

What was it like the first time you jumped?

> At ten minutes out (before the jump) they give you the ten-minute warning and everyone stands. You attach your cord to the cable above your head, so now everyone is standing in a line facing the door. As the countdown continues, your heart starts beating faster and faster. You do this step-drag shuffle thing toward the opening and soon, one by one, you see guys start falling out of the plane. When it gets to be your turn, you hand your cord to the jumpmaster. And go.

How do you make yourself jump out? Does someone ever have to push anyone out?

> The times I've jumped, it's been from a jet. The wind currents are so strong around the plane, all you have to do is stick your foot out and it pulls you out. You don't have to jump... you just stick your foot out. Then as soon as you're out of the plane, there is this incredible, awesome silence. No more engine roars or wind turbulence. It's peaceful, actually. Then, of course, you remember where you are and that there are things you have to start doing to prepare to land. Some people say they have easy landings, but all my landings have been rough!

There's something in this young man's experience that we all can learn from. Is there a "jump" that we need to attempt? A decision we need to make? Something we need to do? A step we need to take? It may be scary, intimidating, even uncertain. We may wonder what will happen, how things will turn out. Regardless, no one (including God) is going to push us out or make us jump. It's up to us.

Whatever it is that we're facing, God will give us the strength and the courage to do what we need to do. We need not worry about the outcome. If God is leading us there, He will take care of us. We can go for it and jump… And if jumping seems just way too impossible, we can simply stick our foot out and let the winds of His love carry us away.

Wide Awake

"I have come that they may have life, and have it to the full."

John 10:10 (NIV)

There is a conversation that occurs between Meg Ryan's and Tom Hanks' characters in Joe vs. *the Volcano*. They are on a boat in the middle of the ocean, and the question on the deck is "Do you believe in God?" In the discussion that follows, Ryan delivers the following lines:

> My father says that almost the whole world is asleep. Everybody you know, everybody you see, everybody you talk to. He says that only a few people are awake... and that they live in a state of constant amazement.

What could her father mean by that statement? Is he right? Are most of us "asleep?" Why would those who are "awake" live in amazement?

It's easy to sleepwalk through our lives... we get up, read the paper, go to work, earn a living, go to the gym, take care of family, spend time with friends, work some more, fall into bed, get up and do it all over again the next day. It's not a bad way to live, but we can miss out on so much!

People who are "awake," notice the miracle and mystery of life... the beauty of creation, the laughter of children, the wonder of silence, the tenderness of relationships, the heartache of disappointment, the necessity of hope, the grief of broken dreams, the heights of love, the rhythms of time, the music of the soul.

In a later scene, stranded on a makeshift raft in the middle of the ocean, Tom Hanks watches the huge moon rise over the horizon. He struggles his sunburned, dehydrated, exhausted body to his feet. With his arms outstretched, he begins speaking until his voice trails off. "Dear God, whose name I do not know. Thank you for my life. I forgot how big you..."

Living our lives wide awake will leave us standing in amazement of the God who created us and who loves us completely.

Keep Shooting The Ball

"And so I tell you, keep on asking, and you will be given what you ask for. Keep on looking, and you will find. Keep on knocking, and the door will be opened."

Luke 11:9 (NLT)

Soon after Rick Barnes became the University of Texas Longhorn basketball coach, his team upset the then-15th-ranked Connecticut Huskies on a Monday night. On national TV. An ESPN "Big Monday" game. It was a huge win for a program that was on-the-rise under Barnes' leadership.

The Longhorns jumped to an early 21-9 lead, but then it was as if someone put a lid on the basket. They only scored twice in the next 10 minutes and ended the first half trailing by one point.

Who knows exactly what Coach Barnes told his team at halftime; but we can guess that along the way he said something like this. "Keep shooting the ball. The shots will start falling. Get good looks at the basket, and keep shooting the ball."

Even the best athletes sometimes get in a shooting slump. They go from their normal play of consistent scoring into a phase where they can't make a basket. Nothing has changed. Same shooting form, same shot locations... even the same lucky socks! But no matter what, the ball will not go through the hoop.

What do you tell an athlete who is in a shooting slump? How do you help her break out of it? "Keep shooting the ball." Even though your confidence slips. Even though you get tired of missing. Even though you want to stop trying. "Keep shooting the ball." It's the only way to get through a slump.

It's not just athletes who go through slumps. We all have those times. We're still doing all the right things, but the payoff isn't there like it once was. For those of us who are in a slump now? The same words are for each of us... "Keep shooting the ball."

> To the teacher who is discouraged by her student's lack of interest... keep teaching.
>
> To the company employee who feels his hard work is unnoticed... keep working.

To the writer who has writer's block... keep writing.

To the attorney who loses a case... keep pursuing justice.

To the parent whose child seems unresponsive... keep loving.

To the alcoholic who craves a drink... keep going to meetings and working the steps.

To the family overwhelmed with grief... keep living.

For those of us who are discouraged, and wonder if what we do even makes a difference, remember... "Keep shooting the ball."

Getting Back on the Plane

"My help comes from the Lord, who made the heavens and the earth!"

Psalm 121:2 (NLT)

In January 2001, an airplane carrying players, staff, and supporters of the Oklahoma State basketball team crashed in Colorado, killing two players and eight other members of the travelling party.

A couple of weeks later, in the first road trip for the team following that tragedy, someone captured a photograph of Jason Keep as he walked around the front end of the plane and intently looked it over before getting on board. It captured what most, if not all, of the OSU team were feeling. Getting back on that plane was probably one of the most difficult things those guys had done in their young lives. It was also probably one of the most healing.

There is something about facing our pain and our fears that is important, that provides healing in a way that no amount of grieving or time can provide.

In *Top Gun*, after Maverick's plane goes down and Goose (his best friend) is killed, Maverick feels responsible and heartbroken. After the review hearing, Viper tells his Lieutenant Commander "Get him up flying... soon." Why? Viper knew that the longer he stayed on the ground, the tougher it would be to fly again.

Another movie, *The Horse Whisperer*, chronicled the journey of Grace, a young horse-rider healing from an accident that left her injured, killed her friend, and traumatized her horse. There comes a moment in the movie when, in order to continue the healing process, she has to get back up on the horse. But it is not without extreme apprehension and great courage.

Sometimes healing requires facing our pain and our fears. It's the child getting back on the bicycle after falling and scraping a knee. It's the athlete coming back after a season-ending injury. It's offering another proposal after receiving a rejection notice. It's daring to love again after a great loss. It's choosing to begin again after yet another failure.

No one would have blamed any of the OSU athletes if they had decided not to fly again. No one would have blamed Maverick for turning in his wings. Or Grace for giving up her love of horses. There are probably things no one would blame us for wanting to leave behind either. But if we're honest, there are probably things we need to do in order to continue healing.

Maybe it's time we step back onto the "plane" in our own lives, and fly once again… knowing that we never fly alone.

Chosen

"For you are a chosen people. You are a kingdom of priests, God's holy nation, his very own possession. This is so you can show others the goodness of God, for he called you out of the darkness into his wonderful light."

1 Peter 2:9 (NLT)

Many young men grow up dreaming about being a part of the National Football League. Then comes Draft Day... the annual two-day event where each team in the league has an opportunity to choose the players they want to add to their team.

It's an anxious and exciting day for young players who have been deemed "draft material" by the media and football community. "Who will pick me?" "Where will I play?" "Will they think I'm good enough?"

Early in the draft when a team announces its selection, the player is greeted and congratulated by the management and/or coaches. He is then presented a team jersey and cap while cameras flash and tapes roll. It's kind of the "welcome to the family" moment.

Little Giants begins with Little League tryouts. It becomes quickly obvious which of the kids are athletes and which ones are not. Still, every kid hopes to make the team. As the team members are announced, the expressions on the faces of the kids tell it all. They want to be on the team. They hope they will be chosen. They live and die with each name that is called. The ones who make the team jump and celebrate. Those who don't stand frozen in disappointment.

We all know the feeling. We all want to be chosen. We long to belong. We wonder if we've got what it takes. We hope someone will want us. We walk through life with the little child inside of us, jumping up and down, hands waving... "Pick me! Pick me!"

The good news is that we have already been chosen. God has written His name of Love across our hearts. We belong to Him. We don't have to prove we are good enough or that we're a worthwhile investment. He wants us on his team.

Deeper Still

(A Prayer of Brokenness and Thanksgiving)

For those of us who inflict pain and suffering

who choose to abuse and destroy

whose selfishness exceeds compassion

whose harmful words and actions bring devastation...

O God we thank you

That as deep as our darkness runs

Your love runs deeper still

and Your grace is sufficient.

For those of us who have been wronged by another

who know what it's like to lose someone

whose dreams have been stolen

whose hearts continue to ache...

O God we thank you

That as deep as our pain runs

Your love runs deeper still

and Your grace is sufficient.

For those of us who watch and listen

who try to make sense of the craziness

who wonder how things got this out-of-hand

who long for redemption, peace, reconciliation...

O God we thank you

That as deep as our hopelessness runs

Your love runs deeper still

and Your grace is sufficient.

We rest in Your love and grace on this day. Amen.

Elbow Room

"Follow God's example in everything you do, because you are his dear children.

Live a life filled with love for others."

Ephesians 5:1-2 (NLT)

Several years ago there was a man who made frequent business commutes from Austin to Dallas via Southwest Airlines. For those of us who have flown Southwest, we know that they have an "open seating" policy. Passengers board by designated groups, but can sit in any seat they so choose.

This particular gentleman always arrived early so as to be in the first boarding group. Once on the plane, he would choose a seat on the aisle. Then he would take the barf bag from the seat pocket in front of him, open it up, and hold it with both hands between his knees. It was amazing how no one ever sat beside him... with the occasional exception of a reluctant and worried passenger imprisoned on a completely full flight!

A funny story. And not a bad idea to gain some elbow room on a flight (if you're gutsy enough to handle the looks and comments that get thrown your way)! But it's a sad story if it reflects a lifestyle.

Some of us live our lives like this gentleman approached his commuter flights. We do whatever it takes to keep people at an arms length. We want our space, our privacy. We don't want anyone to get too close to us. We like travelling alone.

There are advantages to not opening ourselves up to people. We don't get hurt as much. We don't miss them when they're gone. And we are always in control. But it's a lonely lifestyle.

We were not made to be alone; God created us to be together. We need each other by design... with all the good and the bad and the ups and downs. Let us remember that it is by God's love and grace that we are able to let people into our lives. We don't have to navigate things alone. God enables us to live life fully, as both givers and receivers.

A Goofy Investment

"And I, the Son of Man, have come to seek and save those like him who are lost."

Luke 19:10 (NLT)

We know how it is when we get ready to sell something... like, let's say... the house. We do our best to make it look really great. Mow the yard, trim the hedges, make the kids clean up their rooms, shampoo the carpet, light some candles, bake some bread, and on and on it goes. It's like that with anything we want to sell. It's got to look appealing to the buyer.

There was a piece of land for sale once on the north side of Hwy 31 in East Texas. Nice location, numerous trees, country atmosphere. Problem was, with the great amount of rain that had recently fallen, the front half of the property was under water. In fact, the water was just high enough to cover the phone number on the "For Sale" sign by the fence.

Who would need that number? Who would want to put a home on land that always had the potential of going under? Helloooo… time to take the "For Sale" sign down. Wait till the sun comes out, then put the notice up. But expecting someone to make an investment in its present condition… that's *goofy*!

We would like to think we have better judgment than that. Call Him "goofy" if that's what it is, but wouldn't it be just like God to pick up the phone and dial the number?

Paul put it like this:

> When we were utterly helpless, Christ came at just the right time and died for us sinners. Now, no one is likely to die for a good person, though someone might be willing to die for a person who is especially good. But God showed his great love for us by sending Christ to die for us while we were still sinners. (*Romans 5:6-8 NLT*)

Never mind that our behavior, words, and thoughts are not always appealing. Never mind that we have a tendency to get flooded with fear, pride, and worry. Never mind that we might not be the best choice of investments. God still looks at each one of us and says "I want that one." And then He opens his arms and welcomes us home.

Forcing the Issue

"My thoughts are completely different from yours," says the Lord. "And my ways are far beyond anything you could imagine. For just as the heavens are higher than the earth, so are my ways higher than your ways and my thoughts higher than your thoughts."

Isaiah 55:8-9 (NLT)

The toddler-and-mommy morning post-wakeup routine consisted of going downstairs, flipping on a light, kicking up the thermostat, turning on the tap water for the cat to drink (yes, from the kitchen sink), and then choosing the yogurt flavor-of-the-morning from the refrigerator. At some point, usually after making their way into the family room, the toddler would alert his mommy that the cat was finished and the water needed to be turned "off."

Until one morning.

Holding close to his usual timing, the toddler sounded the "off" alert. Then a quick glance toward the kitchen revealed that while the cat had finished drinking, he was still sitting in the sink. A couple of minutes later, same status. A bit frustrated with the unanticipated delay, the toddler decided to take matters into his own hands.

As soon as his mommy stepped into another room, he darted the other way, towards the sink. Arms up, and running and yelling at the cat, he slammed his hands into the cabinet doors below the sink. Mission accomplished. The cat jumped up and scrambled down to the basement.

We, too, get frustrated when things don't go according to our plans or our timing. And the temptation is often great to take matters into our own hands. We run and yell and try to force the issue. Or we quietly scheme and maneuver to accomplish our goal. Whatever our method of choice, we decide to attempt to control the situation.

Some things, however, are beyond our control. Some things, no matter how much we try, cannot be hurried. Some things, as hard as it may be to do, are better left in God's hands.

Today, may God grant us the serenity to accept the things we cannot change, the courage to change the things we can, and the wisdom to know the difference. Amen.

Outside the Comfort Zone

"My grace is enough; it's all you need. My strength comes into its own in your weakness."

2 Corinthians 12:9 (The Message)

What's the big deal about home-field or home-court advantage? Why does it matter on whose turf the business meeting will be held? How is it, that it's always worse to be sick away from home than in your own bed? You guessed it! Comfort. Security. The known variable. A familiar environment. It seems we often function best when we are in an atmosphere that is predictable, a place with few surprises, a situation where we feel in control.

In *Hoosiers*, Gene Hackman (the coach) takes his basketball team into the gym where they will be competing for the state title later that same day. The farm-town team members have never been in such a large arena, much less played ball in one. They are in awe – you can see the fear and doubt start to overcome their faces. Hackman calmly but firmly begins instructing one of the guys to climb on his teammates shoulders and hold a tape measure up to the rim while another teammate reads the tape at the floor. Then he instructs them to measure the distance from the goal to the free throw line.

In a few brief moments, he successfully manages to convince his team that while the surroundings are unfamiliar and overwhelming, the court hasn't changed. The dimensions are the same. The game is the same. Their task remains the same.

We like to stay in our comfort zones, don't we? Whether at work, home, play, or whatever. But some times – and for a million different reasons – we find ourselves in unfamiliar, uncomfortable, even scary places. It's easy to panic or worry or start doubting ourselves. The good news is... it is exactly in those places where we become less dependent on ourselves and more dependent on God. Why? Because we have to! It is in those places outside of our comfort zones that we recognize our need to rely on God and His strength, wisdom, and provision.

When life takes us outside of our comfort zones, may we be thankful... for it is yet another opportunity to grow and be strengthened!

Letter to Santa

"For our hope is in the living God, who is the Savior of all people."

1 Timothy 4:10 (NLT)

A television commercial running during the holidays a few years back, showed a young boy crafting his letter to Santa:

"Dear Santa,

I've been a very, very, very, very good boy..."

Then the boy remembered the time when he let the muddy dogs run through the house. He crossed out one "very." He began to write again, when he suddenly remembered another transgression. He quickly crossed out another "very."

In the next scene, the boy crumples up the paper and tosses it in the trash. He writes a new letter:

"Dear Santa, I have *tried* to be a good boy."

Some of us may see a reflection of ourselves in that commercial. Not in writing to Santa, but in the way we often approach God. We get dressed on Sunday morning maybe. Or find ourselves in the midst of a crisis. Or just decide that it's time to pray.

So we begin our list. We try to convince God how good we've been. We list all the reasons we can think of for why He should bless us or send good things our way. Then we remember. And if we're honest with ourselves and with God, most of us should throw away our list, and simply confess... "we try."

We try. God *knows* we try. We have the best of intentions. We want to please God and live for Him. We want to be reflections of Christ to those around us. We want to do the right thing. But inevitably, we end up getting our houses muddy. Or hurting the ones we love. Or failing miserably.

Which is the whole reason that Jesus came. We all are in desperate need of a Savior on any and every given day.

Bird by Bird

"I can do all things through Christ who strengthens me."

Philippians 4:13 (NIV)

Anne Lamott tells a story in <u>Bird by Bird</u> from which the book received its title:

> Thirty years ago my older brother, who was ten years old at the time, was trying to get a report on birds written that he'd had three months to write. [It] was due the next day. We were out at our family cabin in Bolinas, and he was at the kitchen table close to tears, surrounded by binder paper and pencils and unopened books on birds, immobilized by the hugeness of the task ahead. Then my father sat down beside him, put his arm around my brother's shoulder, and said, "Bird by bird, buddy. Just take it bird by bird."

Sometimes we become overwhelmed by the mountain that is in front of us:

We wonder if it's really possible the recovery and rescue workers will ever get to the bottom of the debris and rubble... they will. Piece by piece.

We wonder if it's really possible to maintain sobriety.... it is. Day by day.

We wonder if it's really possible to complete an assignment... we can. Task by task.

We wonder if it's really possible to heal from a broken heart... it is. Memory by memory.

We wonder if it's really possible to regain lost trust... it is. Little by little.

May God give us the grace to face the mountain that is in front of us, and the courage and strength to live our lives one day, one step, one bird, at a time.

The Presence of God

"I can never get away from your presence! If I go up to heaven, you are there; if I go down to the place of the dead, you are there. If I ride the wings of the morning, if I dwell by the farthest oceans, even there your hand will guide me, and your strength will support me."

Psalm 139:7-10 (NLT)

Help us to see You among us

In the sun climbing over the morning horizon

or the moon hanging in the evening sky

In the leaves on the trees

or the flutter of birds' wings

In the smile on a stranger's face

or the written words from a friend

Help us to hear You among us

In the laughter of children

or the pitter-patter of raindrops

In the noise of the city

or the quiet of solitude

In the conversation between friends

or the words of a song

Help us to feel You among us

In the gentle breeze

or the cool night air

In the arms of a loved one

or the embrace of a child

In the corners of our aloneness

or the community of faith

Open our eyes, ears, and hearts

to know that You are with us

every second of every day

every day of every year

every year of our lives. Amen.

The Script

"We know that all things work together for good for those who love God, who are called according to his purpose."

Romans 8:28 (NRS)

Phil Alden Robinson. A name we might not recognize, but we've probably seen his work. He directed *Field of Dreams*.

After reading and falling in love with the novel, Shoeless Joe, Robinson was convinced a movie needed to be made. It took a long time to sell the idea. As a result of his persistence and passion and belief in the power of the script, Universal eventually agreed to produce it. Robinson recalls his excitement at pursuing his own dream, once the pieces had fallen into place. But even more intense was the pressure he felt to make the project succeed.

About halfway through the filming, Robinson began to get discouraged. He felt like the film was turning out to be okay, but not great. He sensed something was missing. His discouragement deepened into depression. About that time, he received a phone call from his friend and producer, Larry Gordon. Gordon began the conversation:

"Do you still believe in the script?"

"Yeah, I do."

"You're getting depressed at dailies (daily filming/shooting) because you're not seeing magic on the screen. You won't. In a comedy, you go to dailies and you look at things and say, "Okay, that's funny!" In an action, you go to dailies and say "Boy, that explosion is great; that gunfire is terrific!" *This* film, you can't tell from the pieces if it's working. You won't know until it's all put together if it works. All you have to fall back on is the screenplay... and you're shooting the screenplay. Keep at it. Don't lose faith. Keep your eye on the prize and keep going."

Gordon's words of encouragement were healing for Robinson in the making of the film. If we let them, they may be healing for us in the living of our lives as well.

We live the "dailies" of our lives - the events, the relationships, the successes, the failures, the surprises, the tragedies, the joys - and we wonder... How in the world does it all fit together? Where is it going? Does life make sense? The real question we need to ask ourselves is, "Do we still believe in the script?"

If we believe that God's Word is true, we can keep "shooting" one day at a time. We can trust that one day, when all of our stories are assembled together in the big picture, we'll see that it works. For now, all we have to fall back on is the Screenplay and its Author.

But it's enough. Thank God, it's enough.

Never Too Late

"Keep putting into practice all you learned from me and heard from me and saw me doing, and the God of peace will be with you."

Philippians 4:9 (NLT)

True story. Seventeen years ago, Ken Nutter lost his wallet while getting gasoline on his way from New Hampshire to Florida.

It was found by a man named Michael St. John, who tried earnestly to locate Nutter. When his initial attempts did not succeed, he placed the wallet in a safe in his home with the intention of continuing to try to find the owner.

St. John forgot about it until ten years later when he was moving out of his house.... he rediscovered the wallet in his safe. This time, he successfully tracked down Nutter, calling him and telling him that he had the wallet the entire time and had intended to find and send it to him. The wallet soon arrived in Nutter's mailbox, contents intact and a money order for $600 – the amount of cash that had been in the wallet when Nutter lost it.

Sometimes we have good intentions that for one reason or another, get derailed. Eventually, we may decide that too much time has passed to follow through. But the story above reminds us that it's never too late to do the right thing.

> We may think that too much water has gone under the bridge, but it's never too late to make amends.
>
> We may feel that we're too deep in lies, but it's never too late to tell the truth.
>
> We may believe that we've experienced too much pain, but it's never too late
>
> to forgive and be forgiven.
>
> We may think too much time has passed, but it's never too late to say "Thank you."
>
> We may be comfortable with our lifestyle and habits, but it's never too late to stop self-destructive behavior.
>
> We may feel the damage is too overwhelming, but it's never too late to say "I'm sorry."

There are some right things we know we need to do. It's never too late.

This Too Shall Pass

"My thoughts are completely different from yours," says the Lord. "And my ways are far beyond anything you could imagine. For just as the heavens are higher than the earth, so are my ways higher than your ways and my thoughts higher than your thoughts."

Isaiah 55:8-9 (NLT)

This, too, shall pass.

They're probably the last words we want to hear in the midst of tragedy or crisis. "Don't belittle our pain." They're probably also the last words we want to hear in the midst of good times. "Don't remind us it doesn't last."

These four words don't necessarily have to be discouraging ones. In fact, they can be life-giving if we allow them to help us regain a healthy perspective.

In <u>A Cry for Mercy</u>, Henri J. M. Nouwen wrote:

> Lord, life passes by swiftly. Events that a few years ago kept me totally preoccupied have now become vague memories; conflicts that a few months ago seemed so crucial in my life now seem futile and hardly worth the energy; inner turmoil that robbed me of my sleep only a few weeks ago has now become a strange emotion of the past; books that filled me with amazement a few days ago now do not seem as important; thoughts which kept my mind captive only a few hours ago, have now lost their power and have been replaced by others.
>
> Why is it so hard to learn from this insight? Why am I continuously trapped by a sense of urgency and emergency? Why do I not see that you are eternal, that your kingdom lasts forever, and that for you a thousand years are like one day?

Life moves on and carries us with it. Issues that consume our attention now will soon fade and give way to other issues. It's the way life works.

The next time we are feeling overwhelmed by life, may we stop and remember: *This too shall pass.* Each moment of our lives fits into a grander scheme. We are all a players in a bigger picture. And although we can't see or understand the big picture, we *can* find all the comfort and security we need through trusting the One who can.

Getting in First

"God blesses those who realize their need for him,

for the Kingdom of Heaven is given to them."

Matthew 5:3 (NLT)

A day of high fever and a trip-and-fall-down incident after undressing for his bath left the toddler in no mood to get in the tub. He cried and screamed, clinging to his mommy. She set him in the tub and he climbed right back out. Thinking it might just be time to abandon the idea, she looked over to see his dad rolling up his pants legs and taking off his socks.

"What are you doing?" she asked.

"I just thought I'd get in first," he replied.

So he stepped into the tub, with Ernie and Elmo and other bath toys floating around his ankles. They laughed at the silliness of it all and their laughter caught the toddler's attention. "Daddy?" he whimpered, before breaking out into a grin.

"Do you want to join Daddy in the tub?" his mom asked.

"Yeah..."

So his mom set him back in the tub and his dad took a seat on the side. The toddler started playing with his toys and jabbering away. Bath time was on again.

Sometimes, even the things we enjoy can become dreadful. Depression, fear, pain, anger, illness, grief, and more, can take the enjoyment out of things we would normally look forward to. Other times we find ourselves facing things that no one would want to experience, even on the best of days.

So we cry and cling and try to hide. We scramble back to safety. We kick and scream and refuse to move forward. Until we remember: we don't have to go it alone. No matter what we may be facing, we can look up through our tears and see that Jesus is already there... waiting to take our hand and lead us on.

The First Move

"Blessed are the peacemakers, for they will be called children of God."

Matthew 5:9 (NIV)

Before his death in 2005, Pope John Paul II took a journey in which he followed the steps of the Apostle Paul to Greece, Syria, and Malta. When he arrived in Athens, Greece, he became the first Roman Catholic leader to have visited Greece in almost a thousand years.

The division between the Catholic and Orthodox Christians can be traced back to the Great Schism of 1054. Events since then have only served to deepen the divide. The significance of the Papal visit and his prayer for forgiveness in the presence of Greece's Orthodox leader, Archbishop Christodoulos, was monumental.

We know from the news reports that covered his trip, that his attempts toward reconciliation were not accepted by all. Some protested his arrival. Some sneered at his prayer for forgiveness. Some shouted accusations and slanderous remarks.

Regardless of the reception he received, the important thing is that the Pope made the first move and took a step toward healing and reconciliation. As followers of Christ, our journey will required we often take a similar road.

The road toward reconciliation is rarely an easy one. The division between us and another can be deep and painful and old. We never know how our attempts at extending an olive branch or building a bridge will be received. Our pride sometimes prevents us from claiming our contributions to the division. It's often much more comfortable to let it ride.

May we remember that we don't have to know all the answers or how things will work out. The important thing is that we reach out and make the first move.

The "Bug in the Basement"

"Now we see things imperfectly as in a poor mirror, but then we will see everything with perfect clarity. All that I know now is partial and incomplete, but then I will know everything completely, just as God knows me now."

1 Corinthians 13:12 (NLT)

Everyone in the family had been feeling under the weather. It had begun a few days earlier when the first-grader came home from school early one day with a cold and a fever.

"Why is everyone sick?" the six-year-old asked. "Is it my fault?"

"No, it's not your fault," his mom replied. "We probably just caught a bug that's going around."

His thought for a minute before his eyes brightened and he proudly exclaimed. "Now I know! There was a bug in the basement two nights ago while I was playing... I *saw* it!"

We laugh at such a cute – and concrete – conclusion. Perhaps that's because in, it we glimpse a bit of a reflection of ourselves.

Oftentimes, things happen that cause us to ask, "Why?" Death. Adversity. Conflict. Injustice. Abuse. Addiction. Tragedy. And the answers, or lack of them, we get from God don't cut it. They don't meet our acceptable level of understanding. So we quickly come up with our own conclusions that are sometimes as silly as the "bug in the basement" theory.

The truth is, as human beings, our understanding is limited. It's finite. We may never know or grasp the reasons that some things happen. But God, who sees the big picture, "causes everything to work together for the good of those who love God and are called according to his purpose for them." (*Romans 8:28 - NLT*)

Perhaps the most important question we ask is one we ask ourselves, "Will we continue to trust God even when life – and the answers – don't make sense?"

What You Got

"Now glory be to God! By His mighty power at work within us, He is able to accomplish infinitely more than we would ever dare to ask or hope."

Ephesians 3:20 (NLT)

The 18-wheeler pulled past the city bus. On its huge side panel was an advertisement for Goodwill Industries. A picture of a pair of blue jeans, followed by the words, "That pair of jeans you gave to Goodwill just helped somebody land a job."

Marketing and advertising executives recognize the concept that all of us long to be a part of something bigger than ourselves. The ad on the truck not only plays to that, but it also reminds us that the giving of ourselves often results in the satisfaction of knowing that we were able to help someone along the way.

The more subtle message, though, is that we are never truly able to know the extent of our contributions or gifts. And we're not just talking blue jeans or money kind of contributions either. The smile, the note, the offer to listen, the music, the story, the whatever-it-is-that-you're-called-to-do... we never know how someone might benefit from our offerings.

Don't think for a moment that what we have to offer doesn't matter or isn't good enough to give! There is a song written by Billy Crockett and Milton Brasher-Cunningham – "What You Got" – that includes these lines:

> but oh remember
>
> the fish and the loaves
>
> show love has a math of its own
>
> what you got is more than enough
>
> when God gets a hold
>
> of what you got

As we go, may we give of the gifts that God has given us... trusting that in our act of giving, God will get a hold of it and multiply its impact beyond our wildest dreams!

Looking and Moving

"Let us run with endurance the race that God has set before us. We do this by keeping our eyes on Jesus, on whom our faith depends from start to finish."

Hebrews 12:1-2 (NLT)

A beginning motorcyclist is often instructed, "Look where you want to go. Because," they say, "you're gonna go where you look." For example, if a rider is turning a corner or negotiating a curve, looking down into the curve will cause him or her to lay the bike down. Looking ahead and out of the curve gets the rider safely through it.

Farmers follow the same instructions. When plowing a field, the farmer fixes his eyes on an object located on the opposite side of the field and plows directly toward it. The result? A straight line or path. If the plower starts looking around, the rows become crooked and crazy.

"Look where you want to go, because you're gonna go where you look."

Where are we looking? What are we moving toward? If we're always looking back, we'll end up living in the past. If we look around us, we'll end up distracted or stuck. But if we look ahead, we'll continue to move forward.

Paul says our endurance comes from keeping our focus on Christ. For Jesus is the One who both sustains us and moves us forward in this thing we call life.

A Coach's Words

"And I am sure that God, who began the good work within you, will continue his work until it is finally finished on that day when Christ Jesus comes back again."

Philippians 1:6 (NLT)

It was a Little League baseball game played by 10-year-olds. The Braves were ahead going into the last inning. Three outs would produce a win. The coach pulled the catcher out to the mound to pitch the inning, and moved the third baseman in to play catcher.

Well, the Braves defense fell apart and they lost the game. Although several players committed various errors, the catcher was particularly upset with his own mistakes. He felt as if the loss was entirely his fault.

During the team meeting following the game, the coach noticed the catcher's demeanor. He called him by name and asked, "How long have you been playing catcher?" The young man shook his head and shrugged his shoulders. "Wasn't that your first time to play that position?" Then looking around at the rest of the team members, the coach spoke again. "Hey guys... today was his first time playing catcher. Don't you think he did a good job?" The team members nodded and clapped in agreement.

What a nice piece of coaching.

It's easy for some of us to be too hard on ourselves. Too critical. Too demanding. We set high expectations but then get down on ourselves when we don't reach them. We aim for perfection but then beat ourselves up when we make a mistake. For some reason, our best isn't quite good enough for us to accept.

Maybe it's time to stop, and hear the Ultimate Coach call our name and whisper these words in our ears:

"You gave it your best. You did a good job... "

Drawing Straws

"Dear brothers and sisters, whenever trouble comes your way, let it be an opportunity for joy. For when your faith is tested, your endurance has a chance to grow. So let it grow, for when your endurance is fully developed, you will be strong in character and ready for anything."

James 1:2-4 (NLT)

A few years ago, eight guys from the same Texas office went snow skiing in Colorado for the weekend. Only four of them arrived back in Austin as scheduled that Sunday night. It seems that their ticketed flight home was cancelled and there were only four available seats on the next flight out. So they had proceeded to do the only natural and fair thing. They drew straws to see who stayed and who came home!

A comment was made to one of the first four home, "You must have drawn a long straw." His response? "Or a short one... it depends on how you look at it."

He's right. The long straw could have meant getting to come home, while the short straw meant being stuck in Colorado. Or. The long straw could have been equal to getting to spend an extra day in Colorado, while the short straw meant you actually made it back in time for work the next day.

"It depends on how you look at it." A pretty significant statement. And not just for straw-drawing outcomes either. It's a significant statement regarding life in general. How we look at something can make all the difference. It's more than just the "Is the glass half-empty or half-full?" approach. It's a perspective on life.

Here's a question: How do we look at the challenges and crises, interruptions and irritations of our lives? Do we regard them as long straws... circumstances merely to be tolerated, endured, or survived? Or is it possible for us to see them as short straws... opportunites to grow and learn?

We can't control a lot of the things that happen to us. But what we can control is how we respond to what happens to us. And that "depends on how we look at it."

"Paw-Prints" of God

"Praise the Lord, I tell myself; O Lord my God, how great you are!"

Psalm 104:1 (NLT)

There is an early scene in *The Lion King*, where Simba (the young lion cub) has decided that he is ready to be king. In his attempt to be brave – as well as satisfy his curiosity – he gets into trouble and has to be rescued by the lion King (Mufasa, his father).

Later that evening, Mufasa calls Simba over to talk about what happened. As Simba slowly and remorsefully moves toward Mufasa, he steps into what seems to be a hole in the ground. He pauses and glances down. He first sees a huge paw-shaped impression left in the mud by his father. Then sees his own paw, only a fraction of the size of the paw-print. He picks up his paw, looks at it, then places it back on the ground. It is engulfed by the hugeness of his father's. It is almost as if you can see the light come on, as Simba is once again reminded how big and powerful his father really is.

In the father-son "discussion" that follows, we see both the strong and powerful side of Mufasa, as well as the tender and loving side. He addresses Simba with reprimand and grace, discipline and love. It's a nice image of God's dealings with us.

There are "paw-prints" all around us – evidence of God's presence, power, and love. Sometimes we step into them by accident. Sometimes they are so obvious we are almost blown away. But most often, the times we see them happen because we have chosen to stop and pay attention – to be aware enough to recognize them.

May the "paw-prints" we step into today remind us that we are unconditionally loved by a big and amazing God.

The Real Deal

"Yes, I am the vine; you are the branches. Those who remain in me, and I in them, will produce much fruit. For apart from me you can do nothing."

John 15:5 (NLT)

A tenant agreed to take care of his elderly landlady's houseplants while she was away for a couple of weeks. He didn't have the greenest of thumbs, but decided he was definitely capable of following a watering schedule.

On his first trip in, with watering can in tow, he headed toward a potted plant in the corner. To his dismay, there – beneath the beautiful green leaves – lying on the floor were two brown, shriveled, dead leaves. He couldn't believe it... in only just a few days, he had managed to kill one of the plants!

His anxiety was relieved later when the landlady's daughter quietly informed him that her mother kept the dead leaves under the plant on purpose. The plant was artificial, and she thought leaving the dead leaves there would give it the appearance of being real. Her strategy worked!

Some of us go to great lengths to pass things off as the genuine article:

> We smile and say "Fine", when inside we are falling apart.
>
> We lie to mask or cover up, when we don't want to expose the truth.
>
> We accumulate money and stuff to appear successful, when we're really unfulfilled.
>
> We talk enthusiastically of spirituality, when our relationship with God is stale.

Being genuine can be messy. Sometimes we may get flooded and overwhelmed. Sometimes we may go through really dry spells. Sometimes parts of our hearts may wither and ache. But being genuine has its rewards, too. When we dare to be real, we find the opportunity to grow and bloom and develop into the people God created us to be.

Enough

"But those who wait for the Lord shall renew their strength, they shall mount up with wings like eagles, they shall run and not be weary, they shall walk and not faint."

Isaiah 40:31 (NRSV)

An article in a newspaper once relayed the story of a three-month-old kitten in Denmark. It seems that unbeknownst to her owner, the kitten climbed (or fell) into the washing machine. She wasn't discovered until after the cycle had completed. Amazingly enough, the kitten survived! And with a lot of care and nurturing from her owner, was soon back to normal.

Can you imagine what this young kitten endured? Oddly enough, many of us can. We know the feeling of being trapped in an endless cycle of turmoil and spinning. We know what it's like to wonder if we are going to survive. We know the struggle of trying to stay afloat.

Some would say that it's impossible for a kitten to survive such an ordeal. Some would say that it's impossible for us to survive some of the things we have experienced, or may be experiencing even now. The good news is that regardless of our situation, God will give us the strength to endure.

In the weeks following his young daughter's death from Leukemia, John Claypool preached a sermon that concluded with the following (found in <u>Tracks of a Fellow Struggler</u>):

> I confess to you honestly that I have no wings with which to fly or even legs on which to run – but listen, by the grace of God, I am still on my feet! I have not fainted yet. I have not exploded in the anger of presumption, nor have I keeled over into the paralysis of despair. All I am doing is walking and not fainting, hanging in there, enduring with patience what I cannot change but have to bear.
>
> This may not sound like much to you, but to me it is the most appropriate and most needful gift of all... And who knows, if I am willing to accept this gift... maybe the day will come that Laura Lou and I can run again and not be weary, that we may even soar some day, and rise up with wings as eagles! But until then - to walk and not faint, that is enough. O God, that is enough!

May God continue to give each of us... enough.

Compassion in the "Swarm"

By this everyone will know that you are my disciples, if you have love for one another.

John 13:35 (NRS)

For those of us who have witnessed the drama and comedy of a U7 soccer game (under seven-years-old), we understand the meaning of "the swarm." Even though players are actually assigned offensive or defensive positions, once the ball is in play... it becomes chaos. Positions are tossed aside and everyone runs to the ball. Until there is a break in play, five or six little bodies continue to hover around the ball, jockeying for position, trying desperately to move it toward the goal.

Jake played goalie for the first half. He was eager to take the field in the second half since it would be, in his words, "my chance to score!" As usual, the swarm formed immediately after the kickoff. It slowly began to migrate downfield, but not before leaving an opposing player in its wake on the ground. Suddenly, from the back of the swarm appeared Jake. He knelt down on the ground beside the player and asked if he was okay, before grabbing his hand and helping him up. In a matter of seconds, both players were back in the middle of the swarm.

What a great picture of compassion! Jake momentarily set aside his desire to score, so that he could check on – get this – not even his own teammate, but an opposing player!

We all have goals to score, deadlines to meet, things to accomplish, and dreams to achieve. Our lives sometimes feel like one big swarm! It's often easy to remain so focused on our own agenda, that we ignore those around us who have fallen and might be hurting.

May we follow Jake's example, and choose to live a life of compassion and love, even in the midst of the swarm.

Over-the-Hill

"Therefore, if anyone is in Christ, he is a new creation; the old has gone, the new has come!"

2 Corinthians 5:17 (NIV)

Who decided that when we get to be a certain age, we are considered to be "over-the-hill?"

Whoever it was, they forgot to tell Joe Dean. Several years ago in Columbus, Ohio, he bowled his first-ever official 300 score. Yep! The perfect game. 12 strikes in a row. The kicker of it all? He was 87 years old! Here's what Joe had to say about it:

"(After 60 years) I'm still learning the game. I was working on changing my technique when I rolled the 300, and I still want to improve. That's one reason I think I did it."

Isn't that amazing? The guy was 87, still practicing his game, refining his technique, wanting to improve. He didn't know the meaning of "has-been" or "over-the-hill" or "all-washed-up." He was too busy making the most of his life!

Sometimes, regardless of how old we are, it's easy to feel like we're over-the-hill – to feel like we're past our prime – especially when it comes to feeling useful to God for His purposes. We think that we've missed the opportune time to surrender our lives to Him. We should have done it a long time ago. There's no way God could use us now. Look at what we've done. Look at the choices we've made. Look at the circumstances of our lives.

Here's the good news. There are no *has-been's* in the kingdom of God. *Over-the-hill* is not defined. And there is no such thing as *all-washed-up*. Everyone has a chance to live his or her life to the fullest.

Beginning *now*.

Remember, God can use us regardless of our history or our age. He can.... and He does.

The Wax Team

"Every time I think of you, I give thanks to my God."

Philippians 1:3 (NLT)

An interesting feature story was presented during the Winter Olympics broadcast a few years back. It revealed the preparation process for cross-country athletes' skis.

There actually exists a "wax team"... men and women who spend countless hours researching and experimenting in search of the best possible wax for the underside of the cross-country skis, chasing the right combination of ingredients that will cause the ski to glide smoothly across the snow. Other members of the team are responsible for the application process, which can take up to ten hours for just one ski! Who would have known?!?

The team members recognize the importance of their role. One of the members stated, "Without the right equipment, even the best of athletes will not be able to win a medal."

Until now, most of us have never known about the "wax team." Yet without their existence and participation, the cross-country athletes that compete every two years at the the Olympics might never accomplish such feats.

There are "wax team" members in each of our lives. Those people who have worked and given and sacrificed for us. People who have believed in us. People who have helped us grow toward becoming the best we can be. People without whom we would not be the same.

May we remember those human blessings God has placed in our lives... and be thankful.

The Signature of God

"Follow God's example in everything you do, because you are his dear children."

Ephesians 5:1 (NLT)

Immediately following the swearing-in ceremony and inaugural address, the United States President will stop briefly in the Capitol to sign documents that can only be signed after he officially assumes the presidency. He uses a different pen to sign each document, giving each of the pens great value because of the occasion for which they have been used. As the media is quick to point out, "There are many people who would love to have one of those in their collection."

Who knows what those pens sell for! Isn't it amazing? A five-dollar baseball becomes worth more than $300 when it bears the authentic signature of Mickey Mantle or Joe DiMaggio. A print triples in value when it has been signed by the artist. A guitar signed by Eric Clapton brings thousands at an auction. A William Shakespeare autograph (of which only six authenticated examples exist) will bring $50 million!

But here's a thought. God has placed His signature on each of us. He created us... there has never been, nor ever will be, another person exactly like each one of us! Then through Jesus Christ, He has redeemed us. We are of infinite worth because our life bears the authentic signature of God.

Let us go and live this day like the amazing, valuable, children of God that we are!

Grace and Love

"How great is the love the Father has lavished on us, that we should be called children of God! And that is what we are!"

1 John 3:1 (NIV)

He was just out of college and headed overseas to serve in the military. His family gathered at the airport to show him support and say their goodbyes.

He walked over to his little sister, who was about to graduate from high school. He put his arm around her shoulders and guided her away from the crowd. "Be careful when you go to college. There's a lot of freedom. I've been there. I know what it's like. And watch out for some of the guys... they're only after one thing and they'll do anything to get it."

A few months later while overseas, he got a phone call from the states. It was his little sister. Her voice trailed off as she uttered the words. "There's something I have to tell you... I'm pregnant... I found out a few weeks ago. Mom and Dad and I have talked and talked about it. I've decided to keep the baby, but we're not going to get married. The guy is 'not really interested' in being a dad."

He let out a deep sigh. One that understood her pain and heartache. That longed to be present so he could wrap his arms around her. That recognized the challenges ahead. Then he uttered four small, but life-giving, words.

"I love you, Sis."

No I-told-you-so or what-were-you-thinking. No twenty-questions. Just four words."I love you, Sis."

What a great example of the love and grace God has for us! He knows the pain we feel when we fail. He understands the heartache we go through when we mess up. Yet He doesn't abandon us. He doesn't run away. When we come to Him and offer the broken pieces of our lives, He embraces us and utters three words before our name. "I love you."

Smile for the Camera!

"You are all children of God through faith in Christ Jesus."

Galatians 3:26 (NLT)

There is a story about a preschool girl and her father out on the porch of their home watching a thunderstorm. Every time the lightning flashed, the little girl would look over at her dad and say, "Wait!" Then she would run to the edge of the porch, look up at the sky, and smile for a moment. Each time, her father's curiosity grew.

Finally, when he could stand it no longer, he asked, "What are you doing? Why do you keep running over to the edge of the porch every time there is lightning?" The little girl looked at her father and proudly proclaimed, "Because God is taking my picture!"

Child-like? Yes. But what a great perspective and understanding of God's affection for each one of us! To believe that He not only loves, but *likes* us enough to constantly be taking our picture.

One day when He was teaching, Jesus told the crowd, "Unless you become as little children, you will never get into the Kingdom of Heaven." (*Matthew 18:3*) It's difficult to know and understand the depth of such a statement, but one thing we can say...

Maybe it's time we start smiling for the camera!

Prayer for Stillness

"He is our God.

We are the people he watches over,

the sheep under his care.

Oh, that you would listen to his voice today!"

Psalm 95:7 (NLT)

O God,

In this my crazy world

of breaking news

changing seasons

demanding deadlines

exhausting questions

Help me to stop

Help me to be

still enough

quiet enough

long enough

To hear Your voice

whisper my name

and tell me

that I am loved.

Amen.

Remember

"For every time you eat this bread and drink this cup,

you are announcing the Lord's death until he comes again."

1 Corinthians 11:26 (NLT)

Each year after the NCAA Men's Basketball championship game, during the post-game show and interviews, there is the ceremonial cutting-down of the net. One by one, each player climbs the ladder toward the rim, carefully snips off a 4- or 5-inch piece of the net, and holds it up for the world to see. When all is said and done, each team member has his own piece of the net to commemorate the event.

Who knows what each player does with his piece of the net? We can probably safely assume that he has a very special place for it. Somewhere visible, somewhere accessible. Somewhere where every time he sees that several-inch length of nylon rope or holds it in his hands or rolls it between his fingers, he remembers... He remembers the night of the ultimate victory, the sweat and tears and cheers, the special words of affirmation by his coach. He remembers the hard work of the season, the relationships with his teammates and coaches, the hopes and dreams of pursuing excellence.

Jesus gave each of his followers a piece of the net. On the night before His death, they ate the Passover meal together. He took the bread and gave it to His disciples, saying "This is my body given for you; do this in remembrance of me." He did the same with the cup. "This is my blood of the covenant, which is poured out for many for the forgiveness of sins."

Now, every time we come to the communion table to eat the bread and drink the wine, we remember. We remember the passion and agony of our Lord Jesus Christ. We remember the victory He secured for us through His death. We remember the depth of love and grace He has for each of us.

A Balloon Called Anger

"In your anger do not sin; do not let the sun go down while you are still angry."

Ephesians 4:26 (NIV)

Even Jesus got angry. Sometimes it was directed at the people in the crowd who were acting like jerks, or the money-changers in the temple, or the fact that the world had gotten so messed up. Regardless of the cause, even Jesus was not exempt from experiencing anger. He felt it, expressed it, and let go of it.

Some couples promise each other that they will not go to bed at night angry with one another. Paul addressed all of us with a similar set of instructions. So what is the benefit of doing that?

What happens when we inflate a balloon until it bursts? It pops in our face and hurts! The balloon can only hold so much air before something has to give. The anger that we experience is a lot like the air in that balloon. We can only collect so much... carry so much... suppress so much... deny so much... before something has to give. Often, that "something" results in a violent tirade or depression or ultra-defensiveness or hurtful words or self-destruction. And we end up hurting ourselves and others in the process.

The benefit from practicing the above principle is that it causes us to deal with our anger on a daily basis. That way it can't collect and cause harm to us and others. We should consistently – at least at the end of the day – identify the anger we have experienced and let it go by offering ourselves up to God for healing, since most of the anger we feel can be linked to a hurtful experience.

How is our anger balloon today? Is it time to carefully let some air escape?

Nothing Wasted

"And we know that God causes everything to work together for the good of those who love God and are called according to his purpose for them."

Romans 8:28 (NLT)

Winters in the Mid-west can often be quite brutal and rather lengthy. Some years ago, there was an urban neighborhood park, complete with a fenced-in basketball court. As one can imagine, in the summertime, pick-up games and hoop dreams filled the court. But in the cold and snow of winter, it became white, frozen, and abandoned.

Until one day.

Not the type to let opportunities slip away, the neighborhood kids found that if they would shovel the snow off of the concrete, the fire department would come and hose down the court.

Instant hockey rink! An ice-covered surface and snow-bank walls! The kids would come skate and play for hours. What could have remained useless, wasted space, suddenly became a fun, life-giving, dream-inspiring venue.

The winters of our own lives can also be long and brutal. We all have experiences that seem to sit dormant and useless. From painful experiences to regrettable choices, we wonder how anything good could come from those aspects of our lives.

Maybe we can learn from the neighborhood gang... With a little willingness and work on our part, along with help from above, even the "useless" experiences in our lives can be transformed. For with God, nothing in our lives is ever wasted. He is able to bring light even into the darkest of places.

Coming Home

"Have mercy on me, O God, according to your unfailing love;

according to your great compassion, blot out my transgressions.

Wash away all my iniquity and **cleanse** me from my sin."

Psalm 51:1-2 (NRSV)

It seems like our degree of sorrow or contrition is often tied to whether or not we have to suffer consequences, doesn't it? For example, we tend to feel bad about speeding only when we get a ticket. Or the time we really feel bad about cheating is only when we get caught. Tests, taxes... you get the point.

Other times we really grieve our failures and shortcomings. Our choices cause someone to get hurt physically, emotionally, or maybe spiritually... and we hurt, too. If there were anything we could do to erase it or rewind the tape or have a do-over, we would. But we can't.

There is something to be said for caring that we've done wrong. It's possible to get to the point that we don't care anymore. Just like a callous forms on our hands or feet, our heart can go from being super-sensitive to being calloused-hard. That's when we're in serious trouble.

Brennan Manning writes in <u>The Ragamuffin Gospel</u>:

> When the prodigal son limped home from his lengthy binge of waste and wandering, boozing and womanizing, his motives were mixed at best. The ragamuffin stomach was not churning with compunction because he had broken his father's heart. He stumbled home simply to survive.
>
> What a word of encouragement, consolation, and comfort! We don't have to sift our hearts and analyze our intentions before returning home. Even if we still nurse a secret nostalgia for the far country, God falls on our neck and kisses us. Even if we come back because we couldn't make it on our own, God will welcome us.

Emotions are unpredictable. Maybe we think we should feel more remorse over our broken promises to God. Maybe we think God can't forgive us because we can't forgive ourselves. Our longing to be right with God is an indicator of a sensitive heart. We can be thankful for that. Why? Because when we begin to take steps toward home, we find God running to meet us!

The point is that we choose to come home.

The Question of Pain

"All you need to remember is that God will never let you down; he'll never let you be pushed past your limit; he'll always be there to help you through it."

1 Corinthians 10:13 (The Message)

She was only 46 when she heard her husband say it. "Honey, your report wasn't good." She wasn't sure what he was talking about. The biopsy that the dentist had taken earlier in the week had seemed so insignificant – a precautionary afterthought – that she had forgotten about it.

"...the biopsy. It was malignant."

She spent the next six weeks undergoing treatment at the M.D. Anderson Clinic in Houston – five hours away from home. Her family members alternated weekly shifts.

One day following a radiation treatment, she and her pre-teen daughter were walking through back through the halls of the clinic. They passed an elderly woman, seated in a wheelchair, holding her head in her hands and crying. Only a few steps past the wheelchair, she stopped and turned around. "Are you okay?" Through her tears, the woman explained she had lost her glasses. She was alone, frightened, and lost. Her name? "Zula." Together, the three of them retraced the places Zula had been – the x-ray area, the cafeteria, and finally the EKG lab. Glasses found. Mission accomplished.

What began as a simple hunt for glasses developed into a friendship between the two women over the coming weeks. Through their conversations and interactions, Zula discovered her friend's source of hope and strength to face her illness and the struggles that accompany cancer. One day Zula decided that she wanted to follow Jesus, too.

What do we do with the pain that invades our lives? Do we throw ourselves a pity party and allow the pain to defeat us. Or do we choose to learn and grow through it, trusting that God will use it to help others?

May we trust that God is bigger than any pain, disease, crisis, fear, or tragedy that may enter our lives. He will carry us, hold us, and sustain us with His arms of love and grace. And He will use us to help others, too.

The Receiving End of Injustice

"Love is not irritable, and it keeps no record of when it has been wronged."

1 Corinthians 13:5 (NLT)

March 29, 2004. NCAA Women's Basketball Tournament. Norman, Oklahoma.

There should have been 5 more minutes. Overtime. A chance to settle it on the court.

Instead, an unbelievable call by the officials ended Baylor University's hopes of knocking off basketball national powerhouse Tennessee. It was a hard-fought, intensity-filled game that came down to the wire. When the buzzer sounded, the game was tied… until the officials put two-tenths of one second back on the clock and handed Tennessee two free throws. She made them. Game over. Baylor went home, and Tennessee advanced to the Elite Eight.

After the game, the Baylor players stood in stunned silence. Coach Kim Mulkey stood shaking her head in bewilderment, "You've got to be *kidding* me." Fans lingered in the stands in disbelief. Sportscasters on the post-game show were angered and upset. Even Tennessee coach Pat Summit expressed her own displeasure at the ending. *(And this author didn't settle into sleep until 4am!)*

What is it about situations like this that get us so steamed?

We feel for the kids who played their hearts out. We feel for the coaches and fans. We so badly want things to be fair.

But it's deeper than that. We know what it's like to be on the receiving end of injustice. We know the pain, the helplessness, the disbelief. Seeing it happen to someone else touches off those feelings inside of us. The stunned silence. The bewilderment of disbelief. The anger of helplessness. We've been there, too.

There are some things that happen to us that are just wrong. There's no explanation for it. There's no changing it. There's no making it better. It's just wrong. We have to live and deal with it. And eventually let it go.

Jesus knew quite a bit about being on the receiving end of injustice. He knew we would experience it, too. Maybe that's why he issued the invitation:

> "Come to me, all of you who are weary and carry heavy burdens, and I will give you rest." *(Matthew 11:28)*

The next time injustice intrudes into our lives, may we remember Jesus' invitation, and choose to find rest and comfort in His loving arms. He knows all-to-well what it feels like to be wronged. He can help us learn to move forward, too… when the timing is right.

Standards of Measurement

"I command you to love each other in the same way that I love you. And here is how to measure it – the greatest love is shown when people lay down their lives for their friends."

John 15:12-13 (NLT)

The family walked across the restaurant parking lot and piled into the car. It was one of the coldest mornings yet... about 12 degrees. As they were driving away, the six-year-old exhaled and watched the vapor disappear. He then pronounced:

"It's definitely cold, alright. I know it's cold when I can see my breath inside the car!"

Everyone has to have a standard of measurement, right?

When it comes to living, there are many standards of measurement available for subscription...

- higher education degrees
- high salary
- beautiful/handsome spouse or significant other
- championship rings
- GPA or SAT scores
- religious or prominent family
- big house, nice car
- number of Facebook friends/Twitter followers

And the list could go on and on. We often spend a lot of our time chasing things and accomplishments, trying to validate our worth. But who's to say if we really measure up? What is the *true* standard of measurement for our lives?

It's simple, really. It's called "love."

Jesus instructed us to love one another the same way that He loves us. That's a tall order, but one worth pursuing if we really want to make our lives count.

"It's definitely love, alright. We can know we're really living when we love those around us!"

INDEX

Anger – 175

Awareness – 31

Being genuine – 21, 27, 71, 125, 155

Body of Christ – 8, 33, 63, 117, 163, 173

Brokenness – 92, 99

Childlike faith – 15, 61, 85

Chosen by God – 23, 66, 113, 119, 161

Christmas – 31, 73

Comfort – 1, 15, 50, 92, 99, 129, 132, 137, 139, 149, 157, 167, 183

Communion – 173

Community – 8, 27, 57, 71, 117

Compassion – 43, 63, 73, 159

Confession – 33

Contentment – 10

Courage – 33, 71, 103, 107, 110, 127, 135

Death – 35, 101

Discipline – 3

Empathy – 73, 92

Encouragement – 8, 27

Endurance – 17, 107, 132, 157

Failure – 51, 87, 125, 149, 167, 179

Faith – 41, 75, 103, 132

Faithfulness – 3, 6, 53, 59, 81, 143, 145

Fear -1, 51, 57, 59, 75, 103, 110

Forgiveness – 39, 51, 87, 141, 179

Giving – 79, 145

God's light – 177

God's love – 15, 19, 29, 43, 45, 50, 57, 63, 73, 75, 87, 99, 101, 113, 115, 139, 143, 149, 153, 159, 167, 169, 171, 179

God's majesty – 25, 105

God's presence – 1, 85, 97, 110, 129, 139, 153, 157

God's provision – 31, 41, 53, 55, 59, 79, 90, 121, 163

God's timing – 121

Grace – 39, 57, 92, 115, 167

Gratitude – 10, 13, 25, 35, 47, 68, 94, 115, 163

Grief – 35, 55, 73, 87, 101, 110, 115

Guidance – 132, 135, 147

Guilt – 87

Healing – 17, 51, 87, 99, 110, 115, 141, 157, 167, 175

Heaven – 101

Helping others – 43, 92, 145, 159, 161, 181

Honesty – 71, 75, 125

Hope – 17, 73, 75, 107, 113, 135, 137

Hurt – 17, 175

Injustice – 37, 183

Loss – 55

Love – 186

Messy Spirituality – 19, 37, 45, 99, 155

Miracle of life – 68, 94, 105

Opportunity – 57, 135, 145, 151, 177, 181

Pain – 181

Passion – 83

Peace – 1, 50

Persistence – 53, 107, 127

Perseverance – 37, 90, 157

Perspective – 47, 83, 94, 132, 137, 151

Prayer – 13, 50, 77, 115, 171

Purpose – 71, 83, 161, 186

Reconciliation – 141, 161

Redemption – 39, 51, 125, 165, 177

Reliance on God – 10, 37, 53, 79, 97, 123, 127, 141, 143, 157, 161, 171, 181

Repentance – 125, 141, 179

Rest – 15, 29, 50, 183

Salvation – 19, 23, 45, 119, 125, 173

Security – 113, 123, 149

Self-image – 66, 161, 165

Struggle – 21, 29, 45, 68, 90

Surrender – 29, 45

Temptation - 3

Thanksgiving – 13, 25

Trust – 1, 10, 41, 53, 59, 75, 79, 90, 103, 121, 127, 132, 137, 143, 147, 155, 181

Wonder – 25, 35, 47, 94, 101, 105, 129, 153, 169

Worry - 59

Worth – 66, 113, 119, 165, 186